James Harvey Robinson

The German Bundesrat

A Study in Comparative Constitutional Law

James Harvey Robinson

The German Bundesrat
A Study in Comparative Constitutional Law

ISBN/EAN: 9783744666824

Printed in Europe, USA, Canada, Australia, Japan

Cover: Foto ©Suzi / pixelio.de

More available books at **www.hansebooks.com**

PUBLICATIONS

OF THE

UNIVERSITY OF PENNSYLVANIA.

POLITICAL ECONOMY AND PUBLIC LAW SERIES.
EDMUND J. JAMES, Ph. D., Editor.

Vol. III.   WHOLE NUMBER IN SERIES, 10.   No. 1.

THE GERMAN BUNDESRATH.

A STUDY IN COMPARATIVE CONSTITUTIONAL LAW.

BY

JAMES HARVEY ROBINSON, Ph. D.,
Lecturer in European History
in the
Wharton School of Finance and Economy,
University of Pennsylvania.

PHILADELPHIA.
1891.

CONTENTS.

NOTE.

The text of the German Constitution, to which reference is made in the following pages, has been rendered into English, and furnished with a brief historical introduction by Professor Edmund J. James.

See publications of University of Pennsylvania, Political Economy and Public Law Series, Vol. I., No. 7. Philadelphia, 1890.

THE GERMAN BUNDESRATH.

A STUDY IN COMPARATIVE CONSTITUTIONAL LAW.

The chief use and significance of the study of the political institutions of other nations, lies not so much in the acquaintance with these themselves, as in the broader and more accurate view of our own institutions which we thereby gain. We first become conscious of peculiarities in objects long familiar to us through contrast with new and different ones. In recognition of this important psychological principle, that consciousness is intimately associated with and dependent upon contrast, I have attempted to give a picture of an institution quite foreign to our notions of government, not so much for the sake of familiarity with a distant and to us essentially unimportant organ of a foreign State, as to make clearer our notions of our own system.

Of the three great factors of government established by the Imperial Constitution of Germany, the *Bundesrath* or Federal Council, the Emperor, and the *Reichstag* or representation of the people, the Bundesrath is first in order of treatment in the constitution. Whether or no this be an intentional recognition of its preëminence,* certain it is that historically and legally the Bundesrath is the center and core of the existing form of government. Hence a study

---

* "Es ist bezeichnend dass die Reichsverfassung den vom Bundesrath handelnden Abschnitt vor jenen stellt welcher dass Bundespräsidium betrifft."—Seydel im Jahrbuch für Gesetzgebung, u. s. w., III., 274.

of this institution inducts one most quickly and easily into
a knowledge of the entire constitutional system, and furnishes at once an explanation and a justification of many of,
the peculiarities which characterize it.

As the present German Empire is a federation made up
of states which, previous to the formation of the Union,
led an independent existence, each under its appropriate
constitution, we naturally look for a reflection of the pre-
valent ideas of government on which the state constitutions
are based, in the constitution adopted for the federation.
In examining the twenty-five state constitutions, one finds
twenty-two of them to be *monarchical* in form, while the
three remaining ones only, those of the free cities of Lübeck,
Hamburg and Bremen, are *republican*. A prevailing characteristic, then, of the states of the present German Empire,
as distinguished, for instance, from those for which our
constitution was formed in 1787, is that they are each subject to a monarch. Before considering the relation which
exists between the monarchical institutions of the individual states, and the form of the central government, it will
be necessary to consider briefly the constitutional position
of the German princes, for on an understanding of this depends a clear idea of the imperial constitution.

According to the theory of German constitutional law,
the whole power of the state is vested in the monarch.
The various functions of government find their common
center in his person. Without his consent or against his
will nothing in the affairs of state may take place. " *Er
vereinigt in seiner Person die Fülle staatlicher Hoheit und
Macht.*"* This conception of the monarch, however, as

---

* Meyer. Deutsches Staatsrecht, 2 Aufl., 202.

Schulze writes (Preussisches Staatsrecht, 2 Aufl., I., 153): "Das
monarchische Prinzip nach seinem richtigen Verständnisse, nicht in
seiner tendenziösen Verdrehung, wie es zu Zeiten des Bundes im
Sinne des Absolutismus ausgebeutet wurde, verlangt nur : 'dass die
gesammte Staatsgewalt, dem Rechte der Innehabung nach, in der

possessor of the whole power of the state, no longer includes the idea of unlimited right of self-determination in the exercise of it. He is bound to act in accordance with the provisions of the constitution: all his acts must be countersigned by a responsible minister: many of the most important functions of government, especially legislative, can only be exercised in co-operation with the representatives of the people. Still the monarch has both legally and practically the advantage over the people in any movement towards a more popular form of government. He has still the tradition of unlimited power behind him; the restrictions which the constitution has imposed are comparatively recent, in the chief state of the Empire, Prussia, being scarcely more than forty years old. The autocratic conceptions of the former *Bundestag* still linger in the dictum that where a doubt concerning the right to exercise a power arises, the presumption is always in favor of the monarch. This doctrine is, of course, based on the theory that such rights alone fall to the people as have been expressly granted them, all others remaining vested, as heretofore, solely in the monarch.* Over against the monarch the parliament appears simply as an instrument of restraint, limiting him in the exercise of certain of his powers.† In

Person des Staatsoberhauptes vereinigt bleibe, dass keine Funktion der Staatsgewalt von dem monarchischen Mittelpunkt losgelöst werde, dass in allen staatlichen Dingen nichts ohne und nichts gegen den Willen des Monarchen geschehen könne.' "

* " Er [the monarch] behält die Präsumtion der Berechtigung : es stehen ihm alle diejenigen Befugnisse zu, welche ihm nicht ausdrücklich entzogen, den anderen Organen des Staates dagegen nur die, welche ihnen ausdrücklich eingeräumt sind."—Meyer. Deutsches Staatsrecht, p. 202. See also p. 242. Compare Schulze, Deutsches Staatsrecht, I., 477, who expresses a somewhat divergent view.

† "Der Landtag erscheint nicht als Mitträger der Staatsgewalt neben dem Monarchen, sondern als ein beschränkender Factor, an dessen Mitwirkung dieser bei Ausübung einzelner seiner Functionen gebunden ist. Es stehen ihm daher nur diejenigen Rechte zu, welche ihm ausdrücklich beigelegt sind."—Meyer. Deutsches Staatsrecht, p. 242.

it are vested none of the sovereign powers of the state, for
these are one and all attributes of the prince. For example,
no bill becomes law because concurred in by both branches
of the legislative body, even one proposed by the ministry
itself and accepted without amendment by the representatives of the people. The sanction of the monarch first
transforms a bill into a law binding on the subject. To
grant this sanction the monarch is in no way bound; expressed in the usual negative form, he has an absolute veto.
These legal conceptions correspond with the actually existing condition. The government (*Regierung*), *i. e.*, the
prince and his immediate ministers, stand over against the
representatives of the people (*Volksvertretung*) in sharp contrast. The opposition has been mellowed by no such gradual changes as meet us in the history of England. The
German prince *rules* as well as *reigns*. Parliamentary government is unknown, and would in fact ill correspond alike
with the prevailing conditions and the accepted theories.
The ultimate determining factor in the State is not the will
of a party, but the supposedly impartial decision of the
monarch, who is above all parties.* It is significant for the
correct judgment of the relation between monarch and
people that the initiative, although no longer legally,† is
still practically in large measure confined to the monarch.
The "*Regierung*" has taken the initiative so long that it
continues to do so, even under the altered conditions. The

---

* In regard to the possibility of conflict between the Landtag and
the ministry, Schulze observes : "In einem solchen Falle, ist der
Monarch welcher im konstitutionellen Staate über den Parteien stehen
und auch seinem eigenen Ministerium gegenüber eine vorurtheilsfreie
Stellung bewahren soll, recht eigentlich zu einem persönlichen Ein-
greifen berufen, um den Staatsverderblichen Konflikt zu lösen."
Deut. Staatsr., I., 495.

For the opinion of Wm. I. on this point see Sybel: "Die Begründung des Deutschen Reiches," II., 284–5.

† In some of the lesser German states, the iniative is still confined
to the crown.—See Meyer. Staatsrecht, 463.

people are in general satisfied with knowing and opposing
what they do not want, and too little intent on determining
what they do require.*

In view of what has been said, it will not be surprising if
we find the monarchs, as such, playing an important role in
the Empire, as well as in their own dominions. So important and universal a characteristic of the individual States
as the prevailing monarchical form of government could
hardly fail to exercise a marked influence on the form of
the federal constitution. The Imperial Constitution is indeed, as will appear later, based on and interpenetrated by
the monarchical idea. Nevertheless, and in spite of the
title *Emperor* borne by one of the chief organs of State, we
may not regard the present German federation as a *monarchy*. Such a view is from a legal standpoint quite false
and wholly out of consonance with the accepted notions in
Germany itself. *Politically*, the King of Prussia exercises
in many respects an influence analogous to that which
would fall to a monarch of the Empire supposing such to
exist. Legally, however, the Emperor and the King of
Prussia, although the same person, are to be carefully distinguished. The title "Kaiser," which William accepted in
1871, is somewhat misleading, for it is associated with much
that does not belong to the position in the State which it
now designates.† In fact, we have here to do with an en-

---

* See Westerkamp "Uber die Reichsverfassung," 127–8, who criti-
cizes the "wesentlichen negativen Haltung der Landesvertretungen."
He quotes Carl Schurz (p. 128, note) in substantiation of the asserted
difference which exists in this respect between our own country and
the German states.

† Comparing the Roman and the holy Roman Empire with the present German one, Held writes: "Wollte man die Aehnlichkeiten unter
diesen drei Kaiserreichen noch so hoch anrechnen, so müsste man
doch zustehen dass die rechtlichen Verschiedenheiten unter ihnen zu
gross sind, als dass sie unter sich im Verhältniss der Rechtsnachfolge
stehen könnten, da nicht bloss das Recht des Kaisers nach Ursprung
und Gehalt, sondern auch das Object des Kaiserthums in jedem der
drei Fälle im wesentlich anderes ist."—*Das Kaiserthum als Rechts-
begriff*. Würzburg, p. 35.

tirely peculiar political creation, which should not be
judged by previous institutions of the same name, but must
be considered for itself: for it is, strangely enough, *in the*
Bundesrath, and not in the Emperor, that we find the char-
acteristics of a monarch most fully exemplified. This truth
finds its classical expression in Bismarck's famous utterance,
"The sovereignty rests not with the Emperor, but in the
[ideal] unity of the confederated governments." (Die
Souveränität ruht nicht beim Kaiser, sie ruht bei der
Gesammtheit der verbündeten Regierungen.)* Peculiar as
this conception is, it was the product of very easily discern-
ible conditions existing at the time of the formation of the
constitution, and is by no means new. As Laband says, "the
Bundesrath was neither discovered nor invented at the time
of the foundation of the North German Federation, but was
at once a spontaneous generation and a historical fact."†
Some attention to its origin is therefore the first requisite to
an understanding of this most peculiar of all the institutions
of German constitutional law.

In 1814, after Napoleon's forced abdication, the reorgan-
ization of the remains of the Holy Roman Empire became
an object of international solicitude. The first Peace of
Paris touches on this topic in the general provision that
"Les états de l'Allemagne seront independents et unis par
un lien fédératif." ‡ Obviously the serious question of the
manner of reconciling the independence of the members of
the proposed union with the creation of a central power
worthy of the name was here in no way answered. In the
discussion of the new organization of Germany, which took

---

* In the Reichstag, 1871.

† . . . "der Bundesrath [ist] bei der Gründung des Norddeutschen-
Bundes uberhaupt nicht erdacht und erfunden worden, sondern
gleichsam von selbst entstanden, historisch gegeben gewesen."
Staatsrecht des Deutschen Reiches. Zweite umgearbeitete Auflage
(2 Bde.), Freiburg, i. B., 1888. I., 215.

‡ Art. VI.

place at the Congress of Vienna, Prussia's efforts were directed toward the establishment of a firm union, while Austria was intent on the formation of the loosest possible confederation. She had already promised Bavaria and Würtemberg that their newly acquired sovereignty should suffer no diminution, and in these States she found natural and sturdy allies. The empty result of the deliberations was the so-called *Bundesacte*,* or constitution under which Germany lived with a short interruption until 1866. This confederation was officially defined in 1820 as an *international* Union of the German *sovereign Princes* and free cities.† The members of the Confederation were thus not *States*, but *monarchs*. The states found their entire and exclusive representation in the person of their prince. Still the membership was confined to actually reigning sovereigns;‡ it was no personal right of an individual. By way of illustrating this somewhat peculiar conception of the union, it may be pointed out that the number of *states* comprised in the Confederation bore no necessary relation to the number of members, but might, as was actually the case, exceed it. The number of members however could never be greater than that of the States, for, although one prince could rule over several States united in a personal union, no State could be subject to more than one prince.

The sole organ of the Confederation was the Diet, (*Bundestag*) permanently assembled at Frankfort-on-the-Main. The plenipotentiaries who composed this assembly were the

---

* A short description of this constitution is to be found in Sybel, *Begründung des Deutschen Reiches*, I., 48 ff. Also in Meyer *Staatsrecht* 2 te aufl. pp. 84–111, and in Schulze, *Deut. Staatsr.* I., 91–111.

† "Der deutsche Bund ist ein völkerrechtlicher Verein der deutschen souverainen Fürsten und freien Städte." *Wiener Schluss-Acte.* Art. I. Mayer's Corpus Juris Confed. Ger., II., 152.

‡ The exceptional position of the Free Cities, owing to their unimportance, may be passed over, here as elsewhere, without explicit mention.

instructed representatives of the members of the union, strictly responsible to the prince whom they represented for the observance of their instructions. They enjoyed all those rights which belong by the rules of international law to ambassadors, especially that of ex-territoriality when attending the meetings at Frankfort. Thus the Diet was no free deliberative assembly where the members voted according to their individual convictions, but a device by means of which the wishes and opinions of the monarchs might be expressed without the necessity of their personal attendance on the meetings.

The Diet had two distinct modes of procedure, distinguished from one another by the apportionment of the votes among the members of the Confederation and the character of the majority necessary for the passage of a bill. When the assembly met in the form of a select council,* as it did for the transaction of the ordinary business, no member had more than one vote, while the smaller states were grouped into so-called *curiæ*, those comprising each group having but one vote among them. A simple majority sufficed for the passage of a measure. More important matters, such as changes in the constitution, the decision in regard to peace and war, etc., could only be acted upon by the so-called *Plenum*. Here even the most insigificant member of the Confederation had his own independent vote, while in order to give them their appropriate weight, the larger states were assigned more than one. Austria, Prussia, Saxony, Bavaria, Hanover and Würtemberg, for example, each had four votes, then followed five members with three, and three with two, the remaining twenty-four having but one each.† In the Plenum the opposition of a single member sufficed to frustrate the passage of a bill. It is unnecessary to describe this institution more carefully here, as many of its peculiarities reappear in its successor, the Bundesrath.

---

* Known as *Der engere Rath.*
† Bundesacte, Art. VI.

The Confederation, sickly from its birth, dragged out a miserable existence of half a century, until Prussia finally undertook the dangerous operation which alone could render a healthful development possible. On June 14th, 1866, the disagreement between the two great powers, Prussia and Austria, in respect to the disposal of the Elbe provinces, reached a crisis. Under the influence of Austria, the Diet voted to mobilize the troops of the Confederation with the intention of directing them against Prussia. Prussia thereupon declared that the bond of union was broken and the Confederation no longer existed. Its example was followed by many of the other States. In the treaties following Prussia's victory at Königgrätz (Sadowa), the dissolution of the old union was formally recognized by Austria and those states which had not yet done so.* Prussia, which had long been intent on reform, could now realize her cherished hopes without danger of Austrian interference. Her plan for a new union of the twenty-two German States lying north of the river Main, embraced three main points; an increased field of activity for the central government, provision for an executive, and the introduction of a representation of the people, which, as in the individual States, was to control the exercise of certain powers of government.

Just before the 14th of June, Bismarck had sent a circular note to the several States containing the sketch of a constitution, and asking if they would, should the tottering Confederation finally give way, join a new Union on the basis of the plan submitted.† This plan proposed that the new union should comprise all the countries of the old, except those owing allegiance to the Emperor of Austria and the King of Holland; but such parts of Prussia as had been outside the former boundary should be admitted, as well as Schleswig—in short, excluding Alsace-Lorraine, the boun-

---

* Excepting Liechtenstein.

† See Hahn. *Zwei Jahre Preussich-Deutscher Politik*, p. 121.

daries should be those of the present empire. Between many of the articles of this sketch and those ultimately adopted, there is such a resemblance both in matter and form of expression that it may be regarded as the first draft of the North German Constitution.

The first official formulation* of the extent and appellation of the new confederation occurs in the Preliminary Peace of Nicolsburg of July 26th, 1866, where Austria consents to a rearrangement of Germany without her participation, and "promises to recognize the narrower union which His Majesty the King of Prussia is to establish north of the line of the Main, and agrees that the states lying to the south of this line may unite,† the regulation of the national bond with the *North German Federation* (Norddeutscher Bund) being reserved for farther understanding between the parties."‡ This provision was acceded to by all the other States lately at war with Prussia, and the negative conditions for farther progress were insured. The dualism which had determined German history for a half a century was forever done away with. The rock against which Prussia's plans of reform in 1849–50 had suffered shipwreck no longer existed.

The positive results were brought about in the following order. It must be kept in mind that the twenty-two states in question were sovereign and independent countries, and the forms observed were those of *international* intercourse. That no violation of any of these rules took place is a subject of congratulation with German jurists, and it is certainly a matter of no little interest to see how this result was achieved; how of two mutually exclusive ideas, that of independence gave way peacefully and legally to

---

* See Laband. *Staatsr.*, I., 15.

† This plan of a union between the South German states was never carried out.

‡ See Hahn. *Zwei Jahre, etc.*, p. 188.

that of subordination to a higher power. Immediately after the dissolution of the old Confederation, Prussia invited those countries north of the Main, with whom she was on friendly terms, to enter into an alliance with her. Sixteen states acceded, and on the 18th of August, 1866, a treaty was signed at Berlin, which was ultimately agreed to by the other rulers north of the Main, including the King of Saxony and the Duke of Hesse-Darmstadt, a part of whose possessions lay within the proposed boundary. It is this alliance which forms the international foundation on which the North German Federation, and hence the German Empire rests, and it deserves a little more careful consideration even in this short sketch.* Unlike the treaty of confederation in 1815, this was not a perpetual league, but was limited expressly to one year. At the expiration of this term the treaty relations were extinguished of themselves, if, by that time, the purpose of the treaty had not been realized in the establishment of a lasting federation. The contracting parties, after concluding an offensive and defensive alliance, pledged themselves to insure the realization of the ends of the temporary alliance, by means of a constitution based on the draft submitted by Prussia on June 10th, 1866. They agreed to send plenipotentiaries to Berlin to deliberate on the draft of a constitution which should be submitted to a parliament for consideration and ultimate acceptance. This parliament was to be called together by the common action of the allied cabinets, who pledged themselves to order for this purpose an election of representatives of the people on the basis of the election law of 1849. In these two bodies, *i. e.*, the congress of plenipotentiaries of the several monarchs, and the representatives of the people, we have the *beginnings* of the *present Bundesrath* and *Reichstag*.

Obviously no confederation is established by these pro-

---

* Compare Laband. *Staatsr.*, I., 16 ff.

ceedings, for the parties have only agreed to establish one. No constitution is agreed upon, but simply the method in which the constitution is to be brought into being.* About the middle of December the congress of plenipotentiaries met as arranged in Berlin, and in secret session took into consideration a new draft of a constitution submitted by Bismarck, in the name of the Prussian government. This, in an amended form, was submitted to the Reichstag in Berlin, February 24th, 1867. In the speech from the throne† King William said that the allied governments, while adhering to the *approved arrangement of the earlier system*, had agreed on a number of definite and limited alterations, which were not only undeniably necessary, but at the same time lay within the bounds of immediate possibility. The important part which the past played in the German constitution is here clearly recognized. The reforms introduced were strictly limited by the existing conditions. There was no attempt to form a constitution based on abstract principles, as in 1848. Although the ground, as Bismarck expressed it, was ill-adapted for the constitutional structure, it had nevertheless to be utilized. In no institution of the present political organization of Germany, do we find so clear an expression of the various factors which had to be considered by the framers of the constitution as in the Bundesrath. The adherence to the "approved arrangements" of the past comes most clearly to light in the character and organization of this body. Such characteristics of the earlier system as answer the existing requirements are retained. Although no legal continuity exists between the Confederation of 1815 and the new Empire, the Bundesrath is a connecting link between the old and the new. Essentially novel in the constitution submitted to the Reichstag in 1866, was the ad-

* See Haenel. *Vertragsmässige Elemente der deutschen Reichsverfassung*, I., 70, and Laband, I., 17.

† Thronrede: Hahn. *Zwei Jahre, etc.*, p. 497.

mission of the people to a share in the government. Here the precedents furnished by the constitutional development of the individual states were strictly adhered to. In addition, the central government was given increased powers in the regulation of commerce and trade. Important alterations were also made in the organization of the army.* Although Bismarck complained that the representatives of the people, not sufficiently impressed with the "hitherto unexampled unanimity of the rulers of 30,000,000 Germans," as expressed in the draft of the constitution, persisted in presenting amendments, this had the effect of shedding no little light on the nature of the proposed government. The various objections had to be met by the commissioners of the allied governments, and so the gap left by the absence of a report of the proceedings in secret conclave was in a way filled out. The final draft, which the congress of plenipotentiaries hastened to accept on the day of its passage in the Reichstag, while adhering in the main to the original plan,† contained a number of alterations and improvements.‡

The federation was not, however, as yet established. Many of the states had only granted the members sent to the Reichstag the right to *deliberate* on the constitution. The constitution had to be ratified by each state. The cabinets could not legally enter such a union as was proposed, for a radical change in each and every particular state constitution was involved, and such amendments could take place only with the consent of the legislature. In each of the states, the needed alterations were, with a due observance of the legal forms, carried out, and the new Constitution of the North German Federation was published in each of them with the identical provision that the law should go into force on the 1st of July, 1867. Thus

---

* See Laband. *Staatsrecht*, I., 22.

† For an *essential change* see Haenel. *Die organisatorische Entwicklung der deutschen Reichsverfassung*, p. 9 ff.

‡ Laband. *Staatsrecht*, I., 28.

each sovereign and independent country declared its intention to enter the union July 1st. Obviously there is no
room here for a discussion regarding the relative age of
states and union. The states were confessedly the parties
to a contract which resulted on the 1st of July, 1867, in the
formation of a new compound state. It is not to be inferred, however, that because the origin of the union was
contractual, the Constitution of the German Empire is regarded as in any sense a compact between sovereign states.
On the contrary, the tendency of German jurists is to deny
the attribute of sovereignty to the states, and ascribe it to
the Empire alone.* The individual state is even deprived
of the old consolation of believing itself "sovereign in its
sphere," for not only may the power of the central government be easily extended without its consent,† but the
whole theory of a "division of sovereignty," which was
formerly looked upon as the distinguishing characteristic of
a federative system, has of late received some rude shocks,
and is discarded as contradictory and untenable by a number of eminent writers.‡

The new Union was, as we have seen, limited to the
countries lying north of the Main. The considerable kingdom of Bavaria, that of Würtemberg, the Grand-Duchy of
Baden and the southern half of Hesse, which together
form over one-fifth of the present Empire, were as yet completely independent of the North German Federation and

---

* See Laband, *Staatsrecht,* I., 81 ff. Also Meyer, *Staatsrecht,* who
enumerates other authorities, pp. 13 note, 170 and note 6. Prof. Max
Seydel, of Munich, the "Calhoun of Germany," is the most able oppo-
nent of this generally accepted view of the nature of the union. His
thesis is, "Die *einzelnen Staaten sind* der Bund." He has developed
his theory in a little book called, *Commentar zur Verfassungs-Urkunde
für das Deutsche Reich.* Freiburg, i. B. 1873.

† Prussia occupies practically, although not theoretically, an exceptional position in this respect, inasmuch as she possesses a sufficient
number of votes to prevent any alteration of the constitution.

‡ See the interesting criticism in Laband. *Staatsr.,* I., 58 ff.

of each other. The constitution was, however, expressly arranged so that the southern states might be admitted easily and without any alteration of the fundamental law. A simple legislative enactment was declared sufficient, no constitutional amendment being required.* The southern boundary was, so to speak, not yet definitely fixed.† All depended on the attitude of the rulers and people of the southern states, when the long cherished dream of German unity should be realized. Before the great shock came which broke down the barrier of particularism separating the states of the south from the north, an *economic union,* the shadow which the coming empire cast before it,‡ had bound Germany in respect to one great field of interests into a whole. In the "Customs Union" re-established in 1867,‖ she found a much closer and more hopeful unity than that existing under the Confederation of 1815.§ Although short-lived, this organization is of the greatest interest as a link in the chain of development. It was organized on the plan of the constitution of the North German Federation.¶ There was a common organ of the cabinets of the allied states in the Bundesrath of the Customs Union, a general representation of the people in the Customs Parliament. The first was formed by the admis-

---

* Laband. *Staatsrecht,* I., 35. The Cons. provided : " Der Eintritt der süddeutschen Staaten oder eines derselben in den Bund erfolgt auf den Vorschlag des Bundes-Präsidiums im Wege der Bundesgesetzgebung." Art. 79, ¶ 2.

† Martitz. *Betrachtung über die Verfassung des Norddeutschen Bundes,* p. 9.

‡ " Die Verfassung des Zollvereins war der Verfassung des Norddeutschen Bundes so völlig analog, dass sie wie ein Schatten erscheint, den die Reichsverfassung vor sich her warf." Laband, *Staatsrecht,* I., 35.

‖ Hahn. Zwei Jahre, etc., pp. 624 ff.

§ The economic union was preceded by a military one. Laband, I., 34.

¶ Hahn, *Zwei Jahre,* etc., pp. 624 ff.

sion of the plenipotentiaries of the southern States into the Bundesrath of the North German Federation; the Parliament by the admission of the representatives of the people elected in the Southern States into the Reichstag. Prussia presided as in the North German Federation. Laws were passed by a simple majority of both bodies, the old requirement of unity which had existed in the previous Customs Union being abolished. "Thus to a temporary international union was given a constitution borrowed from a true state."*

The short and glorious conflict with France carried on by North and South alike, produced the conditions necessary to change the international union heretofore existing into a real Federation. The Southern States after Sedan sent plenipotentiaries to Versailles to consider with the President of the North German Federation their reception into that body. A treaty between the Federation on the one hand and Baden and Hesse on the other, was concluded at Versailles, November 15, 1870, to which was appended a constitution of the German Federation containing such amendments to the North German constitution as the admission of Baden and southern Hesse demanded. Many of the changes were, however, made out of regard to the future admission of Bavaria, whose wishes were already known.† The example was almost immediately followed by Bavaria and Würtemberg. In all these transactions, the States north of the Main appeared always as a whole. No new union was formed, the old was only extended; *the legal continuity between the North German Federation and the German Empire is complete.*

Although the renewal of the expression "*Kaiser und Reich*," which took place at the suggestion of that unhappy prince, King Lewis II. of Bavaria, did not materially alter

---

* Schulze, *Deut. Staatsr.*, I., 167.

† Schulze, *Deut. Staatsr.*, I., 170.

the constitution, a revision had become necessary for other reasons. The fundamental law of Germany was at this time contained in three separate documents, *i. e.*, the constitution agreed upon by Baden, Hesse, and the North German Federation, November 15th; the treaty between these States and Würtemberg, November 25th, and that between the North German Federation and Bavaria, November 23d. To collect and formulate these scattered provisions into a definite Imperial Constitution was the last act of the magnificent political drama which we have just reviewed.*

The present German Constitution is a somewhat puzzling document. It is in style far inferior to that of our own country; the forms of expression are uncouth and sometimes inexact.† Hence, particularly to a foreigner, many clauses are obscure and misleading.‡ This is due to the process of its formation. The Constitution of the North German Federation came into being just after a great war, coupled with grave internal complications in the Prussian state itself. It was a time when something had to be done; when substance took precedence of form.‖ The revision embracing the changes incident to the enlargement of the Federation by the admission of the Southern States shows little improvement. Consequently one cannot be too guarded in his inferences. It must moreover always be kept in mind that the German Constitution differs from ours in origin, nature and purpose, and therefore no simple comparison of the clauses in the two can serve the purposes of real study. "We must," as

---

* This document has never been altered by formal amendment, although in some points the law has undergone important material changes.

† Haenel, *Organ. Entwicklung*, etc., p. 8.

‡ Haenel cleverly explains several knotty points by drawing into consideration the various drafts which lie behind the present constitution.

‖ Cf. Bismarck in the Reichstag., Apr. 16th, 1869.

Schäffle says, "accustom ourselves to look at every sovereign state in each of its stages of development as a political personality."* Nowhere is this more necessary than in dealing with the German Constitution. In it we find the cherished formulations of political speculation giving way to the demands of the actual. We find a great state springing up from a chaos of weak principalities and taking a commanding place among the powers of the world. Yet a great number of the rules formulated by political writers of the eighteenth century, which played so considerable a part in the formation of our own federal system, are ignored in the present German Constitution. The doctrine of a division of powers, for instance, is neither realized in practice nor accepted in theory. We find no checks and balances; no supreme court empowered with the decision of constitutional conflicts. The representatives of the people do not fall into two houses of legislation; the central power does not in general execute the laws it makes; the federal treasury is largely and purposely dependent on the contributions of the several states. In short, the peculiar conditions existing at the time of the establishment of the union are everywhere reflected in the provisions of the constitution. The old definition of a federation showed itself too narrow, and the jurists of Germany have since been endeavoring to formulate a concep·tion which should correspond to the new political phenom·enon.

In the formation of the North German Federation in 1867, the difficulties to be surmounted and the conflicting interests to be reconciled were by no means inconsiderable. It was necessary to give the requisite form to extremely unmanageable material. The various sovereign states which were to be united contained in all some thirty-three millions of inhabitants, but of these a single one, Prussia,

---

* *Bau und Leben des socialen Körpers*, IV. 411. Quoted by Rümelin.

had no less than twenty-four millions, or four-fifths of the whole number. The other fifth was divided among twenty-one States, of which one only, the Kingdom of Saxony, had a larger population than the city of Berlin (then 702,000). Eight of the proposed members had less than 100,000 inhabitants each.* The difficulties of the situation were appreciably increased by the necessity of considering, in the organization of the union, the future admission of the Southern States. Three distinct, and in many respects conflicting, forces had to be brought into harmonious action. There was, in the first place, the Kingdom of Prussia, one of the great European powers, conscious of a glorious past, strong in present victory, with possessions comprising almost thirteen-fifteenths of the whole territory embraced in the plan of union; in truth, a most unmanageable member for a federation like our own. It seemed destined to occupy a dictatorial position in any possible form of union. The second element to be considered was the particularistic or *monarchical* power in the remaining twenty-one countries. These, as we have seen, were, in general, very limited in extent. Had one, at this time, traveled in a straight line from Fulda to Altenburg, a distance of some one hundred and twenty-five English miles, he would have found himself, on the way, in the dominions of *nine* sovereign and independent monarchs, and have crossed thirty-four boundary lines. Insignificant and scattered possessions do not, however, necessarily imply moderate pretensions. Each of these States possessed a long recognized sovereignty not inferior, from a legal standpoint, to that of Prussia itself. And in spite of the efforts of the educated classes in behalf of unity, these minor governments seem in general to have enjoyed a high degree of popularity among their subjects.† Lastly, the force of public opinion had to be

---

* For these particulars, I rely on Haenel, *Organ. Entwicklung.*, p. 9.

† See Sybel's speech in the Reichstag, 1867. Bezold: Materialien der deutschen Reichsverfassung, I., 583.

considered in the new order. This took the form of a
demand for liberal institutions and a united Germany. On
examining the North German Constitution we find each of
these three forces assigned an appropriate organ. The
presidency of the Federation (*Bundespräsidium*) is united
forever in a personal union with the crown of Prussia. In
the *Bundesrath* the princes of the various confederated
states represent collectively the whole power of the federal
state. In the *Reichstag*, a representation of the German
nation as a whole * exerts, as in the individual states, a
check on the exercise of the powers of government.

As has already been pointed out, the President of the
Federation, or, as he is now called, the Emperor, is not
properly speaking a monarch, for the chief characteristics
of a monarch are quite wanting in his case. He has, for
example, no veto, but *must* promulgate all laws which are
constitutionally passed by the Bundesrath and Reichstag,
whether they are agreeable to him or not. In the Bundesrath, and not in the Emperor, is vested the supreme power
of the state. Where powers, lying within the competence
of the central government, are not explicitly delegated to
other factors of the government, there is always a presumption in its favor, just as in the various constitutional mon-
archies of Germany the prejudice is in favor of the monarch. Among the writers on the subject complete unanimity prevails in denying to the Emperor the title of
sovereign.† The explanation for this lies in the experience

---

* Die Mitglieder des Reichstages sind Vertreter des gesammten
Volkes und an Aufträgen und Instruktionen nicht gebunden. (Cons.,
Art. 29.)

† "In der Literatur herrscht darüber volles Einverständniss, dass
der Kaiser nicht Souverain des Reiches ist ; wenn trotzdem zahlreiche
Schriftsteller das Reich als einen 'monarchischen Bundesstaat' bezeichnen oder ihm einen 'monarchischen' Charakter, eine 'monarchische' Spitz zuschreiben, so wird das Wort nicht im staatsrechtlichen
Sinne gebraucht," Laband, I. 89, note.

The old Holy Roman Empire was legally a monarchy. The charac-

of the past. In 1848-9 the attempt of the Frankfurt convention to make of Germany a constitutional monarchy, signally failed. The effort of Prussia at Erfurt was not more successful, although the title of Emperor was rejected and a college of princes introduced. The essentials of a monarchy were retained, and in spite of all the rights granted to the German princes, they became *subjects* of the King of Prussia.* During the debates on the constitution in the North German Reichstag of 1867, Bismarck, in opposition to a motion to include a responsible ministry in the new system, declared that this could only take place if the new constitution was made monarchial, but this he continued, would involve the *mediatization* of those upon whom the monarchial power was not conferred. "Such a mediatization has, however, been neither conceded by our allies nor aimed at by us. It has been hinted here by some that this could be carried out by force, by others, that it would to a certain extent come of itself . . . . We do not, however, believe this to be true, nor do we expect that any considerable number of the German princes would exchange their places for that of an English peer."† Not only did the princes themselves strenuously oppose anything approaching subjection to the King of Prussia, but their subjects exhibited the particularistic tendencies which Bismarck declares to be inherent in the German character.‡ Hence, if the errors of the past attempts at reform were not

---

ter of the new Empire appears in the title, which is not Emperor of Germany, but German Emperor, thus with no territorial attribute. See Zorn, article *Kaiserthum*, in Holzendorff's *Rechtslexicon* (1881), II., 426.

* See Sybel in the Reichstag, Bezold, *Materialien*, etc., i., 562.

† Quoted by Busch in *Unser Reichskanzler*, i., 59-60. Something in many respects resembling the present Bundesrath had been long a cherished scheme of Bismarck's, as a motion of his in the Erfurt Parliament of 1850 proves. See Martitz, *Betrachtungen*, etc., pp. 50-51.

‡ See Busch, *Unser Reichskanzler*, p. 61, and Sybel, *Begründung des Deutschen Reiches*, II., 334-5.

to be repeated, it was of prime necessity that the self-esteem of the individual states as such should be taken into consideration in framing the new constitution. The members had to be compensated *in kind*, so to speak, for the sacrifices of individual power. The past furnished, as already hinted, an excellent basis on which to found an institution which would realize this end. Prussia had proposed to reform the old Confederation by increasing the competence of the central power, adding a representation of the people, and doing away with the requirement of unanimity, thus, as it were, *building around* the old Bundestag or Assembly of the Confederation. The realization of the plan was of course once for all rendered impossible by the sudden demise of the Bundestag in 1866. An institution closely resembling it, however, in many respects, immediately sprang into being through the treaty above referred to of August 18, 1866, for the commissioners sent by the various cabinets during the winter of 1866–67 to deliberate on the draft of a constitution, composed an assembly corresponding in the main with the former Bundestag,* *i. e.*, a congress of the plenipotentiaries of the allied governments voting according to instructions. This developed rapidly into the Bundesrath of to-day. The conduct of the proceedings was naturally assigned to Prussia, and the King of Prussia invested with the right of convoking and adjourning the *Reichstag*, as the representative assembly was already called. The relations between this council of plenipotentiaries and the representatives of the people, con-

---

* Schulze, *Deut. Staatsr.*, II., 47. A precedent for the Bundesrath is to be found even in the oldest constitution of the Holy Roman Empire, such is the continuity of German constitutional development. "Nur mit veränderten Namen," Schulze writes, "ist der Bundesrath an die Stelle des ehemaligen deutschen Rechstages getreten. Mag man *politische* jede vergleichung unseres Bundesrathes mit jenem viel verspotteten Reichstag von Regensburg zurückweisen, für die Staats rechtliche Konstruktion bietet derselbe überraschende analogien." Staatsr. II., 48.

voked early in 1867, are an exact picture of those which continue to exist between the Bundesrath and Reichstag. The constitution was dealt with exactly as a bill would be to-day. The Bundesrath (*verbündete Regierungen*) prepared the draft to bc submitted to the Reichstag. This was, after certain changes, accepted by the latter body, and returned to the Bundesrath for its final acceptance. "No new organization was demanded. Already existing arrangements, at once the natural expression of prevailing conditions and the reflection of historical facts, had only to be more clearly defined and legally fixed."*

Although the Bundesrath is really a perpetuation of an institution characteristic of a loose international union, we must guard against the inference that the present Empire is to be classed with the Confederation of 1815. The Bundesrath, unlike its progenitor, is not the single organ of a loose confederation or *Staatenbund*, but one of the three great organs of a true federation or *Bundesstaat*,† of a composite state which, in contradistinction to its predecessor, possesses an independent power of legislation and administration and a recognized sovereignty over its members, the individual states. This putting of new wine into old bottles might seem, at first thought, a dangerous experiment. It would appear unlikely that an assembly organized in 1815 in accordance with Prince Metternich's ideas of government would find itself at home in the radically altered surroundings of to-day. Such an apprehension would, however, rest solely on the supposition that the conditions which justified the formation of a body like the old Bundestag no

---

* Laband, *Deut. Staatsr.*, I., 216.

† The definition of the words *Federation* and *Confederation* as found in the Federalist, reflect to some extent the peculiarities of our own constitution, and are not precisely equivalent to the terms *Bundesstaat*. and *Staatenbund* as usually understood. Still it seems unnecessary to introduce new terms, as the existing ones may easily be widened to embrace new political phenomena.

longer existed in 1867. A more careful consideration shows that this supposition is not borne out by the facts. All contradiction disappears if we remember that every historical federation retains in its various members political creations belonging to an antecedent period; for should the states of which the federation is formed lose their identity, the federation would merge into a unitary government.

II

The Bundesrath has, as Laband has clearly pointed out, a double nature, corresponding exactly to the double nature of the Federation. It "serves partly for the exercise and assertion of the membership rights of the individual states, partly as an organ of the Empire; in the latter capacity as an ideal unity."* Accepting Laband's distinction, we shall treat the Bundesrath first in its federative aspect, and secondly as an organ of the state.

Without attempting to decide the involved question whether or no the states of a federation may be rightly termed in any sense sovereign, certain it is that many powers appertaining to an independent state are sacrificed on entering a union. In order to recompense the states for this loss, as well as to insure the continuance of the federation, and prevent a lapse into a unitary state, we find in the existing examples of federations, a participation of the states, as such, in the formation of the governing bodies. Of this our Senate affords an example as well as the Swiss *Ständerath*.† Answering a similar purpose, but differing radically in character and origin, is the German Bundesrath. Here we find the states, or their sovereigns for them, not only participating in the government, but constituting in their totality the *collective sovereiyn* of the Empire.

---

* Laband, *Staatsrecht*, I., 217.

† The *Staatenhaus* of the Frankfurt Constitution of 1849 was a similar institution. Cf. Schulze, *Deut. Staatsr.*, II., 46.

Every member of the Federation is represented in this body, but only members have any right to share in its formation. Alsace-Lorraine, for instance, neither has, nor can have, a vote in the Bundesrath. Its exclusion is not due to any difficulty to be encountered in the appointment and instruction of plenipotentiaries, but to the fact that the territory won from France is not a member of the Union at all, but a province of the Empire. No power intervenes between its inhabitants and the Empire. It is not a *state*, but resembles very closely in position one of our territories.* It would farther be out of all accord with the nature of the institution to receive into the Bundesrath representatives of any class of the inhabitants, or to admit to a seat distinguished individuals or the mediatized princes who formerly ruled over their lands as monarchs.

In apportioning the votes among the various members, the framers of the constitution simply adopted the rule of the former Plenum.† In this way the endless discussion

---

* Commissioners are however appointed by the government of Alsace-Lorraine to participate in the deliberations, but not in the decisions, of the Bundesrath. (Law of July 4th, 1879.)

† The following is a comparison between the *Plenum* as it appeared in the Act of Confederation in 1815, and the existing arrangement of the Bundesrath :

	Plenum.	B'rath.	
Austria	4	....	Excluded from the new Union.
Prussia	4	17	The 17 votes of Prussia consist, in addition to its original 4, of those of the annexations of 1866, i. e., Hannover 4, Elec. Hesse 3, Holstein 3, Nassau 2, and Frankfurt 1.
Kingdom of Saxony...	4	4	
Bavaria	4	6	
Hannover	4	....	Annexed to Prussia, 1866.
Würtemberg	4	4	
Baden	3	3	
Electoral Hesse or Hesse Cassel	3	....	Annexed to Prussia, 1866.
Grand-duchy of Hesse or Hesse-Darmstadt	3	3	
Holstein	3	....	Annexed to Prussia, 1866.
Luxemburg	3	....	Excluded from the new Union.
Brunswick	2	2	
Mecklenburg-Schwerin	2	2	
Nassau	2	....	Annexed to Prussia, 1866.
Saxe-Weimar	1	1	

which any attempt at a new distribution would inevitably have entailed, was avoided. The long-established system had lost the arbitrariness which it once possessed, and become, as it were, the habit of the nation.* The four votes of Prussia were, it is true, more than quadrupled by the annexations of 1866, still this was no deviation from the established principle. Bavaria, however, retained in the empire the two extra votes granted her in the Bundesrath of the Customs-Union, and occupies thus an exceptional position.·

The exercise of rights left by the Constitution to the various members is, in principle, the domestic concern of each state, and so determined by state law. A complete understanding of the Bundesrath is therefore impossible without at least a passing notice of the method of choosing and instructing the plenipotentiaries who form that august

	Plenum.	B'rath.	
Saxe-Gotha	1	⎱ 1	The dying out of the Saxe-Gotha line in 1825 caused a re-arrangement of the little Thüringian states, from which the present duchies arose; Altenburg being the former Heldburghausen family. See Meyer, *Deut. Staatsr.*, 90.
Saxe-Coburg	1	⎰	
Saxe-Meiningen	1	1	
Saxe-Heldburghausen.	1	....	
Saxe-Altenburg........	....	1	
Mecklenburg-Strelitz.	1	1	
(Holstein) Oldenburg.	1 .	1	
Anhalt-Dessau	1	⎱	United in 1863, and now known simply as Anhalt.
Anhalt-Bernburg......	1	⎰ 1	
Anhalt-Cöthen	1		
Schwarzburg - Sonderhausen.................	1	1	
Schwarzburg - Rudolstadt..................	1	1	
Hohenzollern - Hechingen	1 ⎱	....	These principalities united voluntarily with the Prussian State in 1849.
Hohenzollern -Sigmaringen	1 ⎰	....	
Liechtenstein..........	1	....	Excluded from the new Union.
Waldeck	1	1	
Reuss (elder line).....	1	1	
Reuss (younger line)..	1	1	
Schaumberg-Lippe....	1	1	
Lippe.	1	1	
Free City of Lübeck ..	1	1	
Free City of Frankfurt	1	....	Annexed to Prussia, 1866.
Free City of Bremen..	1	1	
Free City of Hamburg.	1	1	
	69	58	

* See Bismarck's speech in Bezold, l. c., I., 649.

assembly. But here arises the question, are the *states*, or their monarchs for them, represented in the Bundesrath? On this point the German jurists are not at one. Meyer and several others assert that "the states in their relations with the Empire, as in the case of the earlier confederation, are represented solely in and through the person of their monarchs."* They therefore deny to the individual states the right to grant to the representatives of the people, by constitutional amendment, any participation in the instruction of the delegates to the Bundesrath.† This, they would consider a violation of the imperial law. Still they admit that the princes have a place in the Bundesrath, not in virtue of a personal right, but only as head and representative of their states, and consequently only so long as they continue in possession of the power of the state.‡ Laband, on the other hand, declares the members of the union to be states and not princes. "*Das Reich ist kein Fürstenbund sondern ein aus den deutschen Staaten gebildeter Staat.*" The prince or his ministry is the natural representative of the state in its relations with an outside power, as formerly with foreign states, so now with respect to the Empire. But there is nothing to prevent the state law from regulating the conditions under which the instructions are given.§ There is nothing in the constitution of the Empire, either expressed or implied, indicative that the instruction of the plenipotentiaries belongs exclusively to the monarch or his

---

* Meyer, *Staatsrecht,* p. 347.

† " Da aber reichsverfassungsmässig im Bundesrath nur die Regierungen vertreten sind, so darf die Instruction landesgesetzlich nicht von einer Zustimmung des Landestages abhängig gemacht werden. Meyer, l. c., p. 355.

‡ Meyer, *Staatsrecht,* p. 347.

║ Laband, *Deut. Staatsrecht,* I., 89.

§ " Die Reichsverfassung normirt lediglich die Abstimmung im Bundesrathe, aber mit keinem Worte die Instruktionsertheilung welche *res interna* jedes einzelnen Staates ist." Laband, l. c., I., 226.

ministry. To a foreigner, especially to an American, it is hard to see why the sovereign should be any freer from constitutional control where the interests of the state as a member of the union are concerned, than in internal affairs. They were not absolute monarchs who confederated in 1866, but monarchs *limited each by a constitution.* Even if they and not the states be represented in the Bundesrath, they are not freed from the constraints to which the increasing self-consciousness of nations has seen wise to submit the individual ruler. Inasmuch, however, as nothing happens in the German states without the monarch's will, it is highly improbable that any law will be passed in the individual states, granting the *Landtag* or assembly of representatives of the people, a voice in the instruction of the plenipotentiaries.*

Although an assembly of instructed representatives of the various members, the Bundesrath is to a certain extent a deliberative body. This arises first from the fact that "*instruction*" is a very elastic term, comprehending many degrees of explicitness. "The instructions may consist in a *carte blanche* or in the most minutely detailed course of action, or even in the requirement that the representative must, before proceeding, procure a special indication of the wishes of his government."† It thus often happens that the members are not supplied with instructions for each particular case, but within certain bounds may vote according to their own judgment.‡ This is most natural in the case of ministers and presidents of the individual

---

* Laband adds most characteristically: "Auch ist nicht zu verkennen dass auch aus anderen politischen Gründen ein solches Gesetz verwerflich wäre, da das Volk in seiner Gesammtheit durch den Reichstag eine Vertretung erhalten hat neben welcher die Volksvertretungen der einzelnen Staaten zurücktreten müssen." *Deut. Staatsr.,* p. 227.

† See Seydel, Holzendorff and Brentano's *Jahrbuch,* III., 277.

‡ Meyer. *Staatsr.,* p. 361.

cabinets, who frequently undertake the task of representing their states. In looking over the names for 1888 we find the cabinets of the individual states largely represented. From Prussia, besides the president of the ministry, the ministers of the Interior, of War, of Finance, etc.; from Saxony, ministers of the Interior and of Finance; from Bavaria the same; from Würtemberg, the president of the cabinet and the minister of the Interior.* Thus the Bundesrath appears not so much in the light of a diplomatic body as of an assembly of specialists.† As a means of communication between the various state governments, nothing could be more convenient and effective. Here the leading men meet together and consider the common policy to be pursued. The process of instruction may easily be reversed. The plenipotentiary by his report may affect the opinion of his government, of which he is often an important member, and so instruct rather than receive instruction from others.‡ Still it is always the will of the state government which asserts itself in the vote. The member of the Bundesrath is never, as in our Senate, a representative of the people of the Empire, but of his state government; his is not the voice of the individual, but of the state. This difference is well expressed by Bismarck in his speech of April 19th, 1871. After referring to the proposed Erfurt Constitution where the member was not bound by instructions, but voted according to his own convictions, he continues, "In the Bundesrath the votes do not weigh so lightly; there it is not Freiherr von Friesen who votes, but the Kingdom of Saxony through him. According to his instructions, he deposits a vote which is a care-

---

* See *Handbuch für das deutsche Reich*, 1888, p. 4 ff.   Up to 1880 the names of plenipotentiaries are to be found in the *Reichsgesetzblatt*.

† "Der Bundesrath ist kein diplomatischer Körper, sondern ein sich aus einer Reihe von Fachmänner zusammensetzendes Collegium." Martitz, *Betrachtungen*, etc., p. 43.

‡ Laband, I., 231, and note 3

ful distillation of all the forces which combine to form the
public life of Saxony. This vote is the diagonal of the
political forces which play a part in the Saxon state. . . .
Analogously in the Hanse towns, in the republican members,
it is the whole weight of a great, rich, powerful and intelli-
gent commercial city which is represented in a vote of the
city of Hamburg in the Bundesrath, not the vote of a citizen of Hamburg who can vote this way or that according
to his convictions. The vote in the Bundesrath should com-
command the respect due to the whole political life of a
member of the Union."

The instruction of the members of the Bundesrath is the
affair of the individual state governments, and not a matter
of which that body takes cognizance. In seeming contradiction to this is the clause in the Constitution, "Unrepre-
sented and uninstructed votes shall not be counted."* This
is not to be taken literally. It does not mean that this is
the penalty for voting without instructions, that the vote
of an uninstructed member is simply neglected.† Nothing
could be farther from the truth. The Bundesrath has
neither the duty nor the right to investigate the nature of
the plenipotentiaries' instructions. That he is plenipotentiary suffices. It never inquires whether a member is voting according to instructions, and it would have no influence
on the validity of the decision if it should be afterwards
discovered that all the members had voted without, or
even against, their instructions. The motives are no more
considered in the Bundesrath than in the House of Representatives. The impracticability of attempting such a
supervision and the paralyzing effect on the work of the
assembly is too obvious to need farther amplification.
The clause of the Constitution above referred to means,
first, that the states are in no way compelled to take part

Reichsverfassung., Art 7., ¶ 3.

† Seydel, Holzendorff & Brentano's *Jahrbuch*, III., 277.

in the proceedings;* and that, farther, a member cannot demand that a vote be deferred because he has no instructions.† That his vote corresponds to his instructions, the plenipotentiary is therefore responsible to his home government alone. His vote is in every case unconditionally binding on the state he represents.

The active participation of the individual members of the Union in the Bundesrath is not confined, as a clause in the Constitution would at first glance seem to indicate, to matters affecting their own state directly or indirectly, but extends as well to measures which relate solely to other portions of the Union. The Bundesrath is the organ of the Empire as a whole, and is in principle concerned only with the whole even where but a portion of the realm is directly affected. The clause referred to reads, "In the decision upon a matter which, *according to the provisions of this Constitution*, is not common to the whole Empire, only the votes of those states shall be counted to which the matter is common (*gemeinschaftlich*)."‡ This refers only to the Southern States, which have been exempted from the action of the federal power in certain departments. They have in certain respects, remained outside the Union, so to speak, and are naturally precluded from interfering with matters which do not concern them, either individually or as members of the Union. For example, the votes of Bavaria and Würtemberg are not taken into consideration in decisions touching the administration of the imperial post

---

* Dissenting from this generally accepted opinion, Zorn claims that "dauernde Fernhaltung eines Staates vom Bundesrath würde überdies wohl die Anwendung des Artikel 19 der Reichsverfassung (Bundesexekution) zur Folge haben müssen." Holzendorff's *Rechtslexikon*, I., 435.

†Laband, *Deut. Staatsr.*, I., 222, 228-9. Meyer, *Staatsr.*, 355. Schulze, *Deut. Staatsr.*, II., 51.

‡ Art. 7, ¶ 4.

and telegraph, nor Baden's in matters relating to the beer and brandy excise.*

We now turn to a consideration of the organization of the Bundesrath as a portion of the constitutional mechanism of the Empire. The form of business in this body is regulated to a certain extent by the Constitution, more specifically by the Rules of Procedure.† The latter has not the force of law, and may be altered at the pleasure of the assembly.‡

The Bundesrath is not a permanent assembly as the former Bundestag was in theory, and the old Reichstag of the Holy Roman Empire was in fact, but is assembled at least yearly by the emperor.‖ It is, nevertheless, distinguished from the ordinary parliamentary assembly by the so-called principle of continuity (Kontinuität), which links each new session closely to the last. For, in contrast to the rules of the Reichstag, business is resumed at the point where it was broken off by adjournment at the close of the preceding session.

Although the Constitution vests the power of summoning the Bundesrath in the emperor, he exercises this power only under important limitations. He may not call the Reichstag together without at the same time summoning the Bundesrath, although it is quite allowable and customary, especially for the preparation of bills to be laid before the representatives of the people, to convoke the Bun-

---

* Constitution Arts. 35 and 52. See Laband, *Deut. Staatsr.*, I., 229–30. Meyer, *Staatsr.*, 359.

† Geschäftsordnung für den Bundesrath; printed 1871 at the Könglichen Geheimen Ober-Hofbuchdruckerei, Berlin, 18 pp. Revised 1880. There is a good account of the contents in Laband, I., 252 ff. The writer was unable to gain access to the original, either at the Royal Library or at the Reichstag Library.

‡ Laband, l. c., I., 252.

‖ Schulze, *Deut. Staatsr.*, II., 64–5, and Cons., Art. 13.

desrath alone.* Moreover, the Emperor is bound to assemble the Bundesrath if one-third of the votes, that is twenty, are in favor of it.†

Each session falls, for convenience, into two periods. The important work, where the presence of the chief plenipotentiary of the larger states is requisite, is condensed into as short a space of time as possible; the remainder of the session being devoted to the transaction of the less important business.‡ Thus the leading statesmen are relieved, and their term of attendance shortened. When we recollect that these men play the chief role in the administration of their respective states, in addition to their duties in the direction of the federal affairs, the necessity of this arrangement is obvious.

The conduct of the business devolves upon the Imperial Chancellor, who is designated by the Constitution as President of the Bundesrath. During the session he appoints the time of meeting, and opens the sittings; all communications from the Reichstag, the motions of the individual members of the Union, and all petitions directed to the Bundesrath, pass through his hands. Such petitions as clearly do not fall within the sphere of the assembly he may reject without farther formality. That only a plenipotentiary of Prussia may be appointed to this position is generally admitted.‖ Hence there are vested necessarily

---

* Cons., Art. 13. James, German Constitution, p. 24.

† Cons., Art. 14. James, German Constitution, p. 24.

‡ Laband, *Staatsrecht*, I., 256.

‖ Meyer, l. c., p. 357, note 7; Haenel l. c., II., 24 ff. That the Chancellor must be a member of the Bundesrath, the wording of the Constitution (Art. 15) clearly implies, inasmuch as it provides for the appointment of any *other* member ("jedes andere Mitglied") of that body as a temporary substitute for the Chancellor. That no other member than a Prussian plenipotentiary may be appointed is deducible from the circumstance that the appointment and dismissal of the Chancellor are vested solely in the Emperor. Should he select any other than one of his own representatives, that plenipotentiary might

in a single person the important functions appertaining to the Chancellor or chief administrative officer of the Empire, to the President of the Bundesrath, and lastly to the leading representative of Prussia, a state to which is allotted not only nearly one-third of the votes in every decision and the determining voice in the case of an equal division, but in several important matters an absolute veto. Whatever judgment we may pass on this peculiar arrangement, by which the head of the Executive Department is at the same time the most important member of the chief legislative assembly, it must not be forgotten that we are dealing with a set of conditions and political traditions wholly different from those of our country. Two things should be noted. First, the principle of the division of powers has not the absolute validity which would make its strict application possible. Even in the early Constitution of Massachusetts, where this principle appears among the inalienable rights of man, the executive was not refused all influence on the legislation. In the second place, the position occupied by the minister of the Emperor is precisely parallel to that occupied by the Emperor himself. As Prussia and the Empire are joined in a personal union, so the office of Imperial Chancellor and that of the Prussian Representative in the councils of the Federation are united in the same individual.

The number which shall constitute a quorum in the Bundesrath is determined neither by the Constitution nor by the Rules of Procedure. Although each member of the Union may send as many representatives as it has votes, its influence in deciding a question is in no way connected with the number of its plenipotentiaries present. One is

---

at any time be recalled by the monarch he represented in the Bundesrath, and thus without being dismissed by the Emperor lose the constitutional qualification for the Chancellorship. See Laband, l. c., I, 351. There is an interesting historical argument in Haenel, l. c., II., 28 f.

quite sufficient to cast the votes of his state, which can not be cast otherwise than as a whole. It would be out of accord not only with the theory of the Constitution, for a state or monarch cannot have two wills at the same instant, but with its express provisions as well,* if the votes were disposed singly.

According to the reports of the sittings, the number attending is very much below the possible fifty-eight, one or two only being present from the larger states, while in the case of the smaller ones a single representative (Stell-vertreter) is chosen to act for several conjointly.†

In general, a simple majority is the only condition for the passage of a measure. In case of a tie, the decision is in favor of the side on which Prussia's votes have been cast. The exceptions to this rule are enumerated below. It is striking that in those cases where more than a simple majority is demanded for the passage of a measure, this limitation never extends to the Reichstag. Here a plurality of the votes is the only condition for the passage of every species of bill.

I. Amendments to the Constitution are looked upon as rejected if there be *fourteen* votes against the change. The history of this apparently arbitrary provision is as follows: According to the North German Constitution, a two-thirds majority of the Bundesrath was necessary for the alteration of the fundamental law. This, on the admission of the

---

* Art. 6. James, German Constitution, p. 21.

† Cf. Laband, I., 223. While each little state generally appoints a plenipotentiary of its own. it has at the same time a substitute (Stell-vertreter) in common with one or more other states. So in 1888 the Plenipotentiary of the two Mecklenburgs was also representative of Reuss ä L. and of Schaumberg-Lippe, while the *Vertreter* of Sachsen-Weimar was appointed to the same office by Sachsen-Altenburg, Coburg-Gotha, Schwarzburg-S., Schwarzburg-R. (no other representative) and Reuss j. L. [Handbuch für das Deutsche Reich, 1888.] Presumably the title "Plenipotentiary" is simply honorary, the *Ver-treter* doing all the work.

Southern States, had to be altered; for otherwise Prussia, whose seventeen votes do not constitute a third of the present number, would have been deprived of its control, and left to the mercy of the other states. The requirement of three fourths, which was accepted in the treaty with Baden and Hesse, and which, expressed in the present negative fashion, would have rendered the modification of the Constitution impossible in the face of an opposition which could muster fifteen votes, gave way to the existing provision as a compromise with Bavaria. Prussia is obviously the only State which can, without the co-operation of any other, prevent a widening of the powers of the central government,* but there are quite a variety of combinations by which four of the lesser states can accomplish the same end. Even three may do so, namely, Bavaria, Saxony and Würtemberg.

II. In certain cases no alteration of the existing law can take place unless Prussia's votes be with the majority in favor of the change. This the German jurists chose to regard not as a veto, but as a deviation from the rule which prescribes a simple majority. Comprised in the class referred to are changes in the military or naval arrangements and in the regulations concerning the customs duties and taxes on certain specified articles.*

III. In regard to the reserved rights of the Southern States it is provided in the Constitution that no modification of these may take place without the consent of the State concerned.† The required consent is looked upon as

---

* From the point of view of the sovereignty of the Empire the exceptional position of Prussia offers a strange anomaly. "Man kann daher nur bedingt von einer ideellen Machtvollkommenheit des Reiches gegenüber den Einzelstaaten sprechen, da eine Aenderung der Verfassung gegen den Willen des einzigen Partikularstaates Preussen vollständig ausgeschlossen erscheint." Rümelin: *Zeitsch. für Gesammt Staatswissenschaft.* Bd. XXXIX, S. 199.

* Cons., Art. 35. James, German Cons., p. 27.

† Cons., Art. 78. There is no corresponding clause in the Constitution of the North German Federation.

given if the vote of the State in question be cast in the Bundesrath in favor of the alteration. The question what the *consent* of the privileged member involves or may involve farther than the vote of the plenipotentiary, has been a subject of discussion in Germany.. The views of jurists are divergent, but it is generally held that even if the acquiescence of the Landtag is not required by the imperial law, as some claim,* the consent of the representatives of the people may be made requisite by a law of the state itself. In spite of the efforts, however, to restrict in this manner the power of the monarch to surrender the peculiar advantages of the state, no bill imposing such a limitation has ever been passed even in the Landtag itself, not to speak of receiving the assent of the ruler.†

IV. Finally, a simple majority of the Bundesrath is not sufficient where a dissolution of the Reichstag is involved. For this the consent of the Emperor is necessary, in addition to that of the Allied Cabinets.‡

The Bundesrath, like other legislative bodies, relies on committees for assistance in the performance of its functions. The organization of these is not left, as is usual, to the discretion of the Plenum or assembly as a whole, but is carefully defined by the Constitution (Art. 8). Seven permanent committees are enumerated, and their composition and appointment more or less completely provided for. In each of these, besides Prussia, at least four members of the Union are to be represented, each state having but one vote. The Emperor, as commander-in-chief of the land and sea forces, appoints the members of the Committee on the Army,‖ and that on the Marine, the members of the

---

* Georg Meyer for instance. *Staatsr.*, 481.

† Cf. references in Meyer, 481, note 25, and Laband, l. c., 115-6, and notes. For a history of the attempts to legislate on the subject, see Seydel; Commentar, 276 ff.

‡ Cons., Art. 24. James, German Constitution, p. 26.

‖ In the case of the Army Committee, the Constitution provides

other five are designated by the Bundesrath itself.* On these devolve respectively the consideration of matters pertaining to the customs and federal taxes, trade and commerce, railroad, post and telegraph, justice, and, lastly,† finance (Rechnungswesen). The duties of the committees are generally confined to the preparation of bills for the Plenum. They may not transact business themselves nor issue orders, but simply report to the main assembly.

An eighth committee provided for by the Constitution occupies a peculiar position. It consists of the plenipotentiaries of the kingdoms of Bavaria, Saxony, and Würtemberg, and two other members of the Bundesrath appointed by that body. This is the Committee on Foreign Affairs. It has in practice failed to take the important place for which it might seem destined, and is chiefly interesting as an illustration of the underlying principles of the German Constitution. One of the most important services of the Bundesrath is, as we have seen, that it furnishes a means of intercommunication between the individual cabinets. Opinions are there exchanged, purposes disclosed, and misunderstandings avoided. The political energy of the different states is in this way correlated and a general unity of action insured: all of which is much more essential in a federal system like that of the German Empire than in one like our own. In the United States the individual state does not, as such, participate directly in the conduct of the affairs of the Federation, whereas in

that Bavaria shall always be represented. The same privilege is insured to Würtemberg and Saxony by Military Convention.

* The Bundesrath satisfies itself with indicating the states which are to be represented in the committee, and does not appoint the members themselves directly. This is not in accord with the Constitution, Art. 8. See Haenel, II., 30, and Laband, I., 264, and note 2.

† Three more permanent Committees have been established since the formation of the Constitution, namely, that for Alsace-Lorraine, one on the Constitution, and one on the Form of Procedure. See on the whole subject the excellent account in Laband, I., 261-9.

Germany the weightiest functions of the federal government devolve upon the state governments. Not only do they as a whole form the most important organ of the central government, but to them individually is intrusted, as a rule, the execution of the federal laws in their respective territories. The committee just mentioned is a part of this system of correspondence. It has nothing to do with the instruction of diplomatic agents, or with the conclusion of treaties and conventions with foreign nations, nor even with the preparation of bills for the Bundesrath. It is there solely for the purpose of receiving communications regarding foreign affairs, which are in this manner brought before the ministers of the chief states, who consult on the ends to be pursued and the means best adapted to reach these ends. In this committee alone Prussia is not represented, for the obvious reason that the Emperor, to whom falls the direction of the foreign policy of the country, is necessarily the source of the information of which the committee is the recipient.*

III.

We have thus far directed our attention to the historical development, the nature, composition and organization of the Bundesrath; it remains to consider its *functions* as an organ of the central government. So soon as the plenipotentiary has cast his vote, this loses its previous connection

---

* This committee was not among those founded by the Constitution of the North German Federation, but was established by the treaty between this Union and Bavaria (Nov. 23, 1870), evidently as a concession to the three kingdoms which were to compose it for their diminished international importance. Of the significance of this committee, Delbrück said in the Reichstag, 1870: " Er wird seinerseits Kenntniss von der Lage der Dinge nehmen und wird in der Lage sein, durch diese Kenntniss, durch Anträge, die er an den Bundesrath stellt, durch Bemerkungen, die er dem Präsidium macht, auf die Behandlung der Politik Einfluss auszuüben." Quoted by Seydel, *Commentar.*, p. 110.

with, and dependence upon the individual state. It passes from the sphere of state law to that of federal law, and becomes a factor in the determination which the Bundesrath reaches as a unit. Hence the decisions of this body do not assume the form of an agreement between the individual cabinets or a majority of them, but are an expression of the will of a simple organ of government. The activity of the Bundesrath is confined to no single one of the departments of government, for it exercises at once legislative, administrative and judicial functions. These we shall consider in the order enumerated.

I. The Bundesrath is pre-eminently a legislative body. Its other functions are, when compared with its part in making the imperial laws, of subordinate importance only. The Constitution provides that the legislative power of the Empire shall be exercised by the Bundesrath and the Reichstag, and that the agreement of the majority of both the assemblies shall be requisite and sufficient for the enactment of a law * The legal equality of the two assemblies in respect to legislation would thus appear to be established. We are indeed very apt to class Germany with the countries which have adopted the bicameral system, and to see in the Bundesrath and Reichstag the upper and lower houses so universally encountered in the existing constitutional organizations of Europe and America. This is, however, a mistake. *The Bundesrath is not an upper house in the ordinary acceptance of the term*, although, as Bismarck has said, it performs in a degree the functions of one.† We have already dwelt on its peculiar composition.

---

* "Die Reichsgesetzgebung wird ausgeübt durch den Bundesrath und den Reichstag. Die Uebereinstimmung der Mehrheitsbeschluss beider Versammlungen ist zu einem Reichsgesetze erforderlich und ausreichend." Cons., Art. 5. James, German Cons., p. 21.

† During the discussion of the Constitution, Bismarck made the following significant declaration : "Es ist mir an und für sich nicht leicht, mir ein deutsches Oberhaus zu denken, das man einschieben

We have found it in no sense a representation of any class of the nation, and formally, at least, in no sense a deliberative assembly. The Reichstag alone in the imperial constitution possesses the attributes of a representative, deliberative body. But while foreign analogies are misleading, within the bounds of the Empire itself, we find a highly satisfactory archetype of the relation existing between Bundesrath and Reichstag, namely, that which has, since the introduction of constitutional government, existed in

---

könnte zwischen den Bundesrath, der, ich wiederhole es, vollkommen unentbehrlich ist, als diejenige Stelle, wo die Souveränctät der Einzelstaaten fortfährt ihren Ausdruck zu finden—das man also einschieben könnte zwischen diesem Bundesrath und diesem Reichstage, ein Mitglied, welches dem Reichstage in seiner Bedeutung auf der socialen Stufenleiter einigermassen überlegen wäre, und dem Bundesrathe und dessen Vollmachtgebern hinreichend nachstünde, um die Classification zu rechtfertigen. Wir würden in der Versammlung nicht souveräne Pairs, Mitglieder haben, die ihrerseits geneigt sind, zu rivalisiren mit den mindermächtigen Souveränen in ihrer socialen Stellung. Der Bundesrath repräsentirt bis zu einem gewissen Grade ein Oberhaus, in welchem Se. Majestät von Preussen primus inter pares ist, und in welchem derjenige Ueberrest des hohen deutschen Adels, der seine Landeshoheit bewahrt hat, seinen Platz findet. Dieses Oberhaus nun dadurch zu vervollständigen, dass man ihm nicht souveräne Mitglieder beifügt halte ich praktisch für zu schwierig, um die Ausführung zu versuchen. Dieses souveräne Oberhaus aber in seinen Bestandttheilen ausserhalb des Präsidiums so weit herunterzudrücken, dass es einer Pairskammer ähnlich würde, die von unten vervollständigt werden könnte, halte ich für unmöglich und ich würde niemals wagen, das einem Herrn gegenüber, wie der König von Sachsen ist, auch nur anzudeuten. Der hauptsächliche Grund aber, warum wir keine Theilung des Reichstags in zwei Häuser vorgeschlagen haben, liegt immer in der zu starken Complicirung der Maschine. Die Gesetzgebung des Bundes kann schon durch einen anhaltenden Widerspruch zwischen dem Bundesrathe und dem Reichstage zum Stillstand gebracht werden, wie das in jedem Zweikammersystem der Fall ist; aber bei einer Dreikammersystem—wenn ich einmal den Bundesrath als Kammer bezeichnen darf—würde die Möglichkeit, die Wahrscheinlichkeit dieses Stillstandes noch viel näher liegen, wir würden zu schwerfällig werden." Sten. Ber., S. 430. Quoted by Seydel, *Comm.*, 99.

the individual German states between the monarch and his Cabinet on the one hand and the Parliament or Landtag on the other.*

In tracing the history of a law through its several stages, the divergence of the German system from the prevailing type of constitutional government becomes even more apparent. We find that the Bundesrath and Reichstag are not even legally on the same footing in the execution of their common task of legislation, and that in practice the pre-eminence of the former body is assured, not only by its inherent nature, but by deep-rooted tradition. First, as to the inception of a bill, the Constitution provides that both bodies may propose bills,† and thus places the two on an equality in respect to the initiative. Neither is limited to a simple veto, nor forced to accept or reject a proposed law as a whole. There is, in short, no legal necessity why a bill should originate, as it usually does, in the Bundesrath. The Reichstag, however, looks to the Bundesrath to take the lead in proposing measures, directing a petition to that body if necessary, respectfully asking that it formulate a bill in accordance with its sentiments and submit it to the consideration of the representatives of the people. This is easily explained. The initiative in the German states was, until comparatively recently, confined to the monarch acting through his cabinet; for the proposing of laws on the part of the Landtag was held to be out of harmony with the monarchical principle.‡ It was thus not only expedient, but absolutely necessary, if the people desired any particular form of legislation, that they petition the monarch to lay a bill before them. This tradition no

---

* "Dem *Reichstage gegenüber* nimmt der ¦Bundesrath nicht die Stelle eines zweiten Factors der Repräsentation (einer ersten Kammer oder eines Oberhauses), sondern diejenige Stellung ein, welche in constitutionellen Staaten die *Regierung* besitzt." Meyer l. c., 351.

† Art. 7 and 23. Cf. Laband, I., 534.

‡ Meyer, Staatsrecht., 463.

doubt lingers in the minds of members of the Reichstag, each one seeing in the Bundesrath the person of the monarch of whom he is a subject, and the wisdom of the leaders of his own state government. This is illustrated by the fact that the Reichstag addresses the assembly associated with it in legislation not as the Bundesrath, but as the "*Verbündete Regierungen*," or, as we may roughly translate it, *allied cabinets*.

As one enters the assembly hall of the Reichstag at Berlin, he is immediately struck by a double row of elevated seats, reaching across the end of the apartment on either side of the president's chair. These are the places reserved for the members of the Bundesrath, who, the Constitution provides,* may appear in the Reichstag to represent the views of their respective governments, and must be heard at any time upon request. Not only do the Rules of Procedure of the Reichstag provide for this emergency, but they go so far as to lay down the rule that, after the discussion of any point is regularly closed, it must be considered as reopened if a member of the Bundesrath asks to speak upon the matter. † The practice has not unnaturally grown up in the Bundesrath of informing the Reichstag, during the discussion of important bills, of the character of the amendments which will be acceded to by the Bundesrath.‡ The preparation of bills, the formulation of their contents and the statement of motives, although not so provided for by law, falls to the Imperial Chancellor and the high government officials under his

---

* Art. 9. Jedes Mitglied des Bundesrathes hat das Recht, im Reichstage zu erscheinen und muss daselbst auf Verlangen jederzeit gehört werden, um die Ansichten seiner Regierung zu vertreten.

† Geschäftsordnung, § 48. "Nimmt ein Vertreter des Bunderathes nach dem Schlusse der Disküssion das Wort, so gilt diese aufs neu für eröffnet."

‡ See Laband I., 537, note 5.

control.* It is thus apparent that, while the Reichstag is
legally quite free to exercise its power of initiative, the
preponderance of the Bundesrath is not only indicated by
the provisions of the Constitution, but confirmed by practice. In the final stage of the law making, however, in the
so-called *Sanction*, the ascendency of this body appears
even more clearly.

Every law, we find on analysis, to consist of at least two
easily distinguishable elements, the rules or provisions of
which the *bill* consisted before it became a law ; secondly,
the command or order which renders the observance of
these rules incumbent upon the citizen. The latter element,
or that which converts a bill into a law, is the Sanction. It
is obvious that the rules, which form the content of a law,
may be derived from many sources. They may be suggested
by a minister, by a committee, or even indirectly by some-
one wholly outside the government organization. The
specific effect of the power of the state appears, not in the
formulation of the bill, but in the *sanction* alone, in the
binding force which it may bestow upon any rule of conduct
by which that rule is made law.† In the individual members of the Empire the monarch is invested with the
supreme power of the state, and, although he is not free to
determine the character of a law without the coöperation
of the representatives of the people, he alone can convert
a bill into a law. The question presents itself, to which
of the organs of the imperial government does this
exalted prerogative belong? The answer would seem to
be at hand. All the imperial laws begin with the
formula, "We . . . by the Grace of God German Emperor,
King of Prussia &c., ordain herewith the following." The
power of sanction seems thus to be assumed by the Emperor. But this formula, taken as it is from the Prussian

---

* Laband, I, 533.

† This subject is treated with great care in Laband, 515 ff.

constitution, is not applicable to the Empire. The authorities on the subject agree that the supposition that the power of sanction is vested in the Emperor is neither in harmony with the theory of the Constitution nor with its specific provisions. For the right to exercise this power implies the right to refuse to exercise it at will. The obverse side of the sanction is the absolute veto. As we have seen, the monarchs of the individual German states possess both these powers; strictly speaking both aspects of the single power of sanction are apparent in their case. The Emperor, however, has no veto. The Constitution says explicitly that the agreement of the two assemblies is *sufficient* for the creation of a law. The Emperor *must* publish all laws constitutionally passed, whether he be in accord with their provisions or no. The article which gives him, as King of Prussia, a veto in the Bundesrath on proposed changes in the military arrangements, would be without significance if, as Emperor, he possessed this power in all cases. It is the Bundesrath, not the Emperor, who sanctions the laws.* That this is entirely in harmony with the principles on which that institution is based, as developed in the preceding pages, is obvious.† The sanction of the Bundesrath may appear as a separate act or in conjunction with, and indistinguishable from, the simple approval of the contents of a bill. The Constitution makes it necessary that *every* decision of the Reichstag shall be acted upon by the Bund-

---

* Laband, 542, and note 1 ; Haenel, II., 52 ; Meyer, 472 ; Schulze, II., 118.

† See Laband, 541 : "Träger der souveränen Reichsgewalt ist die Gesammtheit der deutschen Staaten, als ideelle Einheit gedacht. Nur von ihr kann daher der eigentliche Gesetzgebungsact, die Sanction der Reichsgesetze ausgehen. Die Gesammtheit der deutschen Landesherren und freien Städte ertheilt den Entwürfen zu Reichsgesetzen die Sanction, welche sie in Reichsgesetze umwandelt. In allen Fällen aber, in denen die deutschen Bundesglieder ihren Antheil an der Reichsgewalt auszuüben haben, ist der *Bundesrath* das dafür verfassungsmässig bestimmte Organ, nicht der Kaiser."

esrath, *even if it be the acceptance, as a whole and unchanged, of a bill originating in the Bundesrath itself.** The Bundesrath might legally refuse its assent, just as the monarchs of the various members of the union may, even to a bill which it had itself formulated. In this second acceptance of its own approved measures we have the sanction of the Bundesrath distinctly separated from the other aspects of its legislative activity. The analogy of the position it occupies to that of the individual German monarchs is clear, for the Bundesrath has a veto as well as they. It is always legally possible for it to refuse its assent at the last moment to every bill. The act of sanction is not, however, mentioned explicitly in the Constitution, and politically it is almost wholly devoid of significance. It is, nevertheless, of no little importance from a legal and theoretical stand·point, to determine who is the real law-giver of the Empire.

But the legislative activity of the Bundesrath is not limited to the laws passed in conjuction with the Reichstag. Very important measures may take the form of *ordinances*, issued by the Bundesrath alone. The ordinances fall into two distinct classes, which must be carefully distinguished. They may, on the one hand, be simple administrative measures affecting the government officials only. Those to whom they are directed are bound to obey them, not as subjects of the Empire, but as employees of the government. These administrative ordinances will be again referred to in connection with the administrative functions of the Bundesrath. In sharp contrast to these, are those which modify or supplement the law of the land, and bind the subject as such. These are in their nature legislative enactments, and differ from an ordinary law in their origin only. They want the usual qualification of a law, inasmuch as they are created without the concurrence of the representatives of the people. This is obviously a grave defect, so grave as

---

* Meyer, 472, and note 3. Laband, 512.

to make a legislative ordinance a complete anomaly in a
constitutional system based on the division of powers.
For, however free the administration may be to conduct its
own affairs, it must act in a constitutional system within the
bounds of the law. The laws must, however, according to
the modern ideas of government, be made with the concurrence of the people, acting through their representatives—
this in Germany as well as elsewhere—hence, any divergence from this rule must have strong legal justification.
The German Imperial Constitution grants no general power
to any of the organs of the state to enact laws under the form
of ordinances,* but on the contrary says explicitly that the

---

* Art. 7, 2, of the Constitution reads, "Der Bundesrath beschliesst
. . . über die zur Ausführung der Reichsgesetze erforderlichen allgemeinen Verwaltungsvorschriften und Einrichtungen, sofern nicht
durch Reichsgesetz etwas anderes bestimmt ist." This clause is subject to various constructions. Does it give the Bundesrath any right
to issue *legislative* ordinances? If so, to what extent? Meyer claims
that the article does not refer simply to administrative ordinances, but
that the "*Ausführungsverordnungen*" may be, although rarely, legislative ordinances (p. 485, and note 12, also p. 466, and note 8). Loening (Verwaltungsrecht, p. 229) says, "Sofern die Unterthanen aber die
Gesetze auszuführen haben, können durch Verordnung auch Vorschriften über die Art und Weise der Ausführung an sie gerichtet werden."
This species of ordinance would be a *law* according to *Laband*, and
could not legally be issued under Art. 7, 2. Laband's narrower
construction of the clause in question is very fully and ably supported
in his great work, I., 595, ff. In controverting Arndt (*Verordnungs-
recht des deutschen Reiches*, Berlin and Leipzig, 1884) he sums up their
points of difference as follows : "Arndt erkennt aber . . . dass die
Verordnungen des Bundesrathes sich *intra legem* halten müssen, d. h.
nur zur *Ausführung eines Reichsgesetzes* dienen dürfen, und dass die
Befugniss des Bundesrathes stets auf eine Delegation zurückzuführen
sei. Nur hält er nicht eine *specielle* Delegation in dem einzelnen Gesetze
für erforderlich sondern er erblickt in dem Art. 7, Abs. 2 der Reichsverfassung eine *generelle* Ermächtigung auch zum Erlass von Rechts-
vorschriften. Da es nun üblich geworden ist, in allen Reichsgesetzen
die dazu irgend Veranlassung geben, specielle Ermächtigungen zum
Erlass von Ausführungsvorschriften zu ertheilen, so ist die praktische
Differenz zwischen der von Arndt verfochtenen Lehre und der hier
vertheidigten, nicht so bedeutend, als es vielleicht den Anschein hat"

legislative functions shall be exercised by the Bundesrath
and Reichstag, and that the assent of both bodies shall be
requisite to the passage of a law.   Even the power of enact-
ing temporary laws in special emergencies, when the ordinary legislative bodies are not in session, a power commonly
exercised by the monarch of the individual German state,
is unknown to the Empire.*   These general provisions do
not, however, prevent a *delegation* on the part of the usual
factors of legislation of a specified portion of their power to
other organs of the Government—to the Bundesrath, the
Emperor, the Imperial Chancellor, or even to the individual state administration.   Such a delegation, although
quite foreign to our conceptions of the nature of constitutional restrictions, is not only recognized by the eminent
authorities of Germany, but is, as we shall see, sanctioned
by a long series of precedents of unquestionable legal
validity.†   The laws which contain delegations of this character usually designate the organ which shall exercise the
power; if not, the duty devolves upon the Bundesrath.‡
The law-making, which takes the form of ordinances, is

(p. 596, note 4).   The Bundesrath has, however, exercised its power
of issuing ordinances with a freedom which does not appear to be justified by the Constitution.   Both Arndt and Haenel (II., 80–81) have
brought together a number of instances of this character.   Laband,
while rejecting many of the cases as beside the point, admits that the
remainder prove, "dass die Praxis eine schwankende und der Bundesrath nicht in allen Fällen der ihm durch die Verfassung gezogenen
Schranken sich klar bewusst gewesen ist" (p. 599).

* Meyer, pp. 469 and 486, and Schulze, §§ 188 and 288.   "Nach
Reichsstaatsrecht müssen, wie Laband sagt, alle Gesetze im materiellen Sinne auch Gesetze im formellen Sinne sein."   Schulze, II., p. 123.

† "Ein Gesetz kann demnach anstatt *unmittelbar* Rechtsregeln auf-
zustellen, Anordnungen darüber enthalten wie gewisse Rechtsregeln
erlassen werden sollen. . . . Eine vielfach bethätigte Praxis deren
Rechtsmässigkeit niemals weder vom Reichstage noch vom Bundesrathe oder der Reichsregierung angezweifelt worden ist, hat dieser
Auffassung angeschlossen."   Laband, p. 600.

‡ Meyer, p. 485.   Laband, p. 600, note 4.

generally, if not always, a sort of secondary legislation that fills in the details of laws of which the general character has been already determined by the joint action of the two assemblies.* Within the limits already outlined, the Bundesrath, or other organ of state to which the power is specifically delegated, proceeds to amplify the general provisions by a process which Laband compares to the development of a sketch into a painting. Obviously there is scarcely any limit to the extension of this delegated power, nor to the importance of the secondary legislation in modifying the law as it comes from the representatives of the people; in other words, the sketch leaves a considerable latitude for the coloring and *chiaroscuro*. The number of laws which grant the power of secondary legislation to the Bundesrath is considerable. Haenel mentions thirty-five in eleven years.† All laws relating to the customs and taxes, and most of those affecting the financial and industrial interests of the Empire, are of this class.‡

Properly to judge this system, so far as the Bundesrath is concerned, two things must be kept in mind; first, the variety of functions assumed by the German state, and, sec-

---

* For example, the so-called Dynamite Law of 1884 is to be inapplicable to explosives generally used for ammunition. The law does not specify what shall be included in the category mentioned, but delegates the determination of this to the Bundesrath.

† Studien, II., p. 85.

‡ Laband, p. 601, note 1. The delegated power of issuing ordinances may be more or less limited. Sometimes a law provides that the ordinances issued in accordance with its provisions must receive the assent of the Reichstag. In other cases, they must be *submitted* to the Reichstag, which is at liberty to demand their repeal. Ordinances of the former class can be repealed only with the forms of law, while those of the second category may be revoked by the power issuing them, independently of the Reichstag. (See Meyer, p. 486.) The right to issue ordinances is very frequently delegated to the Emperor, acting either independently or with the knowledge and consent of the Bundesrath. For a list of the laws containing delegations of this character see Haenel, II., 76-77.

ondly, the peculiar character of the Bundesrath as already
described. The German Constitution, like our own, has a
" general welfare " clause. Everything, however, depends
on the construction put upon a somewhat vague formula.
It is unnecessary to say that views prevail in the Empire
widely divergent from those traditional in the United
States. " The whole activity of the state," writes an eminent authority on German administrative law, "has for its
end and aim the promotion and development of the national civilization and culture." * This is not too broad a
statement of what would be known in our country by the
question-begging epithet, "government interference." The
administration in Germany has assumed such proportions
as to give rise to a new and important branch of public
law. The field is thus altogether too considerable for a
popular assembly, consisting even of the best qualified
members, to be able in every case to formulate a law, complete in its details and yet adapted to the exigencies of the
occasion. Obviously those called upon to conduct the administration learn better than any one else the rules according to which it is most expedient to act. The laws which
determine the limits of their activity must, while insuring
the rights and liberties of the subject, hamper as little as may
be the administration in the accomplishment of its very
comprehensive ends. The representatives of the people
may content themselves with a general determination of the
limits of a series of legislative measures, leaving the details
to more competent hands, the Bundesrath or the Emperor;
in other words to those organs of state which conduct the
administration. The Bundesrath, although in the main a
legislative body, has, as we shall see, important administrative functions as well. Not only this, but its members are
as we have noted, the heads of the administration in the in-

---

* " Die gesammte Thätigkeit des Staates hat die Förderung der
Kulturentwicklung des Volkes zum Zweck." Loening, *Verwaltungsrecht*, p. 3.

dividual states, men versed in affairs, specialists qualified, if any one, to judge of the form a law may best take in order to realize its ends. Thus a power which, if delegated by our Representatives to the Senate, would be at once unconstitutional and inexpedient, is in Germany, owing to the complexity of the functions of state and the peculiarity of the chief legislative body, both in accord with the system and necessary to its success.

The Bundesrath is an organ of the administration, but not in the sense that it may interfere directly, through specific orders addressed to the government officials. On the contrary, the actual carrying out of administrative measures devolves either upon the Emperor or his representatives, or falls within the scope of the self-administration of the individual state governments.* The term *administration*, is not, as has already been implied, applicable solely, or even chiefly, to the simple execution of the laws. It is a much broader word, including everything which remains, after setting aside the legislative and judicial functions of government.† It is the conduct of the government business in a country where nothing is foreign to the sphere of government regulation. The administration may not only do what it is explicitly empowered to do by law, but everything which is not forbidden by law.‡ It is the free activity of the government within thebounds of law.‖ The cases in which the Bundesrath may exercise administrative

---

* Laband, I., p. 256. Schulze *Deutsches Staatsrecht*, II., p. 56.

† This negative definition is adopted by Meyer : "Unter der Bezeichnung *Verwaltung* fasst man die gesammte Thätigkeit der staatlichen Organe welche nicht Gesetzgebung und nicht Justiz ist zusammen," p. 515.

‡ "Die Verwaltung ist keine blosse *Ausführung der Gesetze* sondern ein *Handeln innerhalb der gesetzlichen Schranken*. Die Verwaltung darf nicht bloss dasjenige thun, wozu sie durch Gesetz ausdrücklich ermächtigt, sondern alles was ihr nicht durch Gesetz untersagt ist." Meyer, p. 521.

‖ The precise nature of the administration from a legal and philo-

functions may be altered by new laws from year to year. There are thus no absolutely determined limits to its sphere of action, deducible from the condition or the nature of the assembly itself. The following classification gives, however, a very just view of the range of its activity.*

According to the express provision of the Constitution,† the Bundesrath decides upon the general administrative measures and arrangements necessary for the execution of the imperial laws, unless that function be delegated by law to some other organ. The individual laws generally provide specifically for the exercise of this power, and, although often delegating it to the Emperor, his minister, or the state governments, the practice has been to leave the determination of the general rules for the administration to the Bundesrath.‡ This class of ordinances must, of course, be distinguished from those already described, which are really laws in the form of ordinances.

Farther, the Bundesrath "decides upon defects" which may appear in the execution of the imperial laws or the administrative measures and arrangements mentioned above.∥ This clause is very awkwardly expressed, and hence difficult to construe, but it is at least obvious that the Bundes-

---

sophic standpoint is the subject of much discussion in Germany. Laband's plausible theory (Staatsrecht, I. pp. 671, ff) is criticised by Haenel in his most recent essay *Das Gesetz im formellen und materiellen Sinne*, (p. 81, ff.) The best known general treatments of the administrative law are those of Prof. Loening of Halle (*Deutsches Verwaltungsrecht*, 1 vol.), and of Prof. G. Meyer of Heidelberg (*Deut. Verwaltungsrecht*, 2 vols).

* For this classification see Laband I., p. 236, and Schulze, *Deut. Staatsr.*, II., p. 56.

† Art. 7, 2. Der Bundesrath beschliesst . . . über die zur Ausführung der Reichsgesetze erforderlichen allgemeinen Verwaltungsvorschriften und Einrichtungen."

‡ Laband, I., p. 237.

∥ Cons., Art. 7, 3. James, German Cons., p. 22.

rath is not to "decide upon the defects," as the Constitution reads, but to provide for their remedy. The remedy in case of a law which proves inapplicable to the existing conditions, would, of course, take the form of a bill to be laid before the Reichstag for the alteration or repeal of the undesirable measure. If the defect were confined to the administrative ordinances issued by the Bundesrath alone, it could alter them as it saw fit. There is, however, a farther signficance in the clause, which may be inferred from its history.* From its origin it is clear that it forms the correlative of the article† which vests in the Emperor the duty of *overseeing* the execution of the imperial laws. The Constitution, in defining the competence of the Empire, (Art. 4),‡ does not, as might be expected, designate a certain number of departments which shall fall to the federal, as distinguished from the state governments, but limits the competence of the federation, in the first instance at least, to the "*oversight and legislation*" in the matters enumerated in the article. This is very striking. Oversight takes precedence of legislation. Of the execution of the laws when made, nothing is said. The execution of the laws made by the federal government is left to the states. The fundamental difference which here presents itself between our system and the German, is pertinently expressed in the definition of a federative government which a recent German writer has put forth: "*If,*" he says, "*we wish to gain an accurate conception of a Federation* (Bundesstaat), *as distinguished, on the one hand from a loose Confederation* (Staatenbund), *on the other from a unitary government, we must vest in the unity of the federated states, the sovereignty, and the regulation of the law. The final exercise of the sovereign*

---

* Laband, I., p. 138.

† Art. 17. James, German Cons., p. 25.

‡ "Der Beanfsichtigung seitens des Reiches und der Gesetzgebung desselben unterliegen die nachstehenden Angelegenheiten."

*power, that is, the immediate execution of the functions of the
state, must, however, in order to maintain the existence of the
individual states, be vested in the said states, under the oversight of the Union..* This definition, while adapting itself
to the German Empire, obviously excludes our own Union
altogether. Its significance lies, however, not in its general
applicability, but in its réflection of the underlying characteristics of the government we are considering. The Empire is sovereign. Many functions of the state are specifically subject to its legislation, and it may increase the field
of its legislative activity, virtually almost at will. On the
other hand, the individual state, within the bounds described
by the Empire, may carry out the laws in accordance with
its traditions, adapting the mode of execution to the local
peculiarities of its situation.† It is the right and the duty
of the federal government always to have a thorough
knowledge of the manner in which its administrative bodies
conduct their business."‡ To the end that it may satisfy
itself that the state governments are fulfilling their constitutional duties, the right of oversight is given it. It is the
Emperor's duty to appoint such officials as are requisite
for collecting the necessary information.‖ Any reported
cases of imperfect execution of the federal laws are laid
before the Bundesrath for consideration. The Bundesrath,
therefore, decides upon the proper interpretation and application of the laws, so far as it is necessary, in order to obvi-

---

* Rümelin: "Das Beaufsichtigungsrecht des deutschen Reichs."
Zeitschrift für die gesammte Staatswissenschaft. (1883.) Vol 39,
p. 202.

† Rümelin, l. c., p. 211.

‡ Das Reich hat vor allem *das Recht und die Pflicht* von der Ge-
schäftsführung seiner Verwaltungs-Körper *eine eingehende* und voll-
kommene Kenntniss zu nehmen. Rümelin, l. c., p. 213. See also
Laband. I., p. 705.

‖ The Emperor may demand reports from the state governments on
their method of conducting the administration of federal laws. Laband, I., p. 707.

ate the concrete difficulty which has made itself apparent. The issue of orders through which the decision of the Bundesrath is executed belongs, however, to the Emperor.* The "defects" under consideration may consist in an erroneous interpretation of the Constitution, the laws, or the administrative ordinances of the Empire, from which results a wrong application of their provisions, or in a tardy execution, or even in a refusal to carry out the laws on the plea that they are unconstitutional.† This important function of the Bundesrath is exercised, it must be remembered, by the leading statesmen of the individual states, who conduct the administration at home. The Bundesrath cannot, however, annul a decision of the state officials, nor issue any orders to the said officials.‡ Its power extends no farther than determining the general duty of all the states, as exemplified by the decision of the case in hand.

The farther powers of the Bundesrath which relate to the administration, (such as the influence it exercises on the nomination of certain officials,‖ as well as the part it plays in the determination of certain peculiarly important matters, such as the declaration of war,§ the conclusion of treaties,¶ the dissolution of the Reichstag,** (where the Emperor may act only with its consent,) inasmuch as they are easily assimilated to the arrangements existing in most constitutional governments, need not be considered here.

The so-called "Execution" (*Bundesexekution*) merits,

---

* See Schulze, II., pp. 56 and 57. Laband, I., p. 241.

† Thudichum. Holtzendorff's Jahrbuch, vol. I., 22, note 2.

‡ "Der Bundesrath bildet keine Instanz über den Centralbehörden der Einzelstaaten so dass an ihn im Wege der Beschwerde oder des Recurses der einzelne Fall zur definitiven Entscheidung gezogen werden könnte." Laband, I., 242.

‖ For the list see Laband, I., p. 243.

§ Cons., Art. 11, 1. James, German Cons., p. 24.

¶ Cons., Art. 11, 2. James, German Cons., p. 24.

** Cons., Art. 24. James, German Cons., p. 26.

however, a few words, as it is wholly foreign to our institutions. The German Constitution provides that in case the members of the union do not fulfil their constitutional duties toward the federation, they may be forced to perform them by means of the "execution," The Bundesrath determines upon the "execution," which is carried out by the Emperor. This is all that is said on the subject, and it seems at first sight a very insufficient treatment of so important a matter as the coercion of the states, the *pis-aller* in a federal system. This simple statement takes the place of a more extended one in the constitution of the North German Federation of 1866, which in its turn suggests the elaborate provisions in relation to the "execution" contained in the fundamental law of the preceding German union.* The diminished clause of the present constitution reflects, to some degree at least, the changed relations of the federal members. There is, perhaps, an unconscious admission that the existing distribution of power is more potent than legal formulas.† Naturally an execution directed against Prussia is out of the question. On the other hand, the Emperor, to whom two million soldiers are bound by oath to execute unconditionally his commands, will scarcely find himself obliged to mobilize a single regiment to carry out the decrees of the Bundesrath.‡

"*Ce qu'un étranger comprend avec le plus de peine aux Etats-Unis c'est l'organization judiciaire,*" ‖ writes De Tocqueville. Similarly, one of the most puzzling departments of German constitutional law for us is that which relates to the Judiciary. Our supreme and inferior courts play such an important constitutional role in our federal

---

* Wiener Schlussakte von 1820, Arts. 31 and 34, and the *Exekutionsordnung*, 1820.

† Seydel, *Comm.*, p. 138.

‡ Thudichum. Holtzendorff's Jahrbuch. Vol. I., p. 28, note 1.

‖ Démocratie en Amérique, I., 163.

system that we are apt to infer that a judicial organization, at least analogous to our own, is a necessity of every federal government. The Imperial Court at Leipzig, however, although a court of last resort, exercises no influence comparable to that which the highest tribunal of the United States exercises on the development of the constitutional law of the union.* The attempts which have not been wanting to introduce a system in some degree resembling our own, have failed.† The Reichsobergericht is not, like the Supreme Court at Washington, one of the great organs of the central government, included in and forming a vital part of the original plan, but first came into being some years after the formation of the union. ‡ But who, then, interprets the Constitution? How is the boundary line separating the province of the federation from that of its members, defined and maintained? To answer these questions a long excursus would be necessary, for the most fundamental differences between our legal traditions and those of Germany are here involved. Suffice it to say that the insignificant role played by the Imperial Court in the formation of the constitutional law of the federation is attributable, mainly, to four peculiarities which distinguish the German Union from our own, viz., the long established monarchical institutions, the peculiar composition of the Bundesrath, the facility with which the competence of the Empire may be enlarged, and, lastly, a much lower estimation of the significance of judicial decisions in comparison

---

* Schulze observes (Deut. Staatsr., II., 59) that the Courts may decide constitutional points *incidentally*. The insignificance of their decisions in this re pect may be judged by the fact that but two or three cases are, so far as my knowledge extends, ever cited as shedding any light on the constitutional law.

† The constitutions proposed in 1848-9 contain elaborate provisions for a Supreme Court, although differing essentially from our own. The federal jurisdiction is, for example, extended to constitutional difficulties arising in, and confined to, the individual states.

‡ 1879.

with free philosophical reasoning which prevails in Germany.*

The jurisdiction in constitutional questions is not delegated to the courts, but, so far as it is provided for at all, it is exercised by the Bundesrath. That this body, whose members vote *according to instructions*, is as ill adapted to perform *judicial* functions as one can well imagine, is clear.†

Nevertheless, by general consent, the Bundesrath is pitched upon as the proper organ to exercise any important function which seems to lie outside the sphere of the other constituted powers. Hence it acts as judge when no other judge is forthcoming. Something has been said already of the judicial activity of the Bundesrath in its decisions concerning defects in the laws or their administration. This often involves an interpretation of the laws, but rarely does their determination take the form of an actual

---

* The following quotations show the strong repugnance which is entertained by some of the ablest thinkers in Germany towards any interference of the courts in cases of alleged unconstitutional action on the part of the federation. . . . " Es musste als ein gerade zu unertiäglicher Zustand angesehen werden, wenn Gerichte ein ordnungsmässig verkündetes Gesetz bei der Entscheidung concreter Rechtsfälle für nichtig erachten, während Kaiser, Bundesrath und Reichstag es als verfassungsmässig zu Stande gekommen aufrecht erhalten" (Laband, I., 556, note 1). Haenel, Laband observes farther on, " erblickt gerade in dem richterlichen Prüfungsrecht der Verfassungsmässigkeit der Reichsgesetze einen *indirecten Rechtsschutz des Einzelstaates* gegen rechtswidrige Eingriffe des Reiches in seine Rechtsordnung. Die Einzelstaaten würden um denselben nicht zu beneiden sein ; denn sie könnten in die eigenthümliche Lage kommen, dass der Bundesrath von ihnen die Durchführung eines Reichesgetezes verlangt und sie mit Bundesexecution bedroht, während die Gerichtshöfe dasselbe Reichsgesetz für nicht nach Massgabe der Reichsverfassung erlassen und deshalb für unanwendbar und nichtig erklären (558, note 3). Farther, see Bismarck on the interpretation of the constitution by the courts, quoted in Busch, *Unser Reichskanzler* I., 32. Radically different views are met in Haenel, *Studien*, I., Chap. V., particularly p. 268 ; also Westerkamp, *Ueber die Reichsverfassung*, 184, ff. Both the latter are familiar with our institutions.

† Martitz, l. c., 37.

decision of the specific case which gave rise to the discussion, as that may have been determined long before. The decision of the Bundesrath serves simply as a guide to those to whom the decision of the case in question, or similar cases, is intrusted.* In a few instances, however, determined by special laws, decisions of the Bundesrath, or its committees, are in nature precisely those of an administrative court ; for example, deciding whether, and to what extent, the gates of a fortress may be widened in the interest of traffic.† The three cases particularly enumerated in the Constitution, in which the Bundesrath is called upon to perform judicial functions, are as follows :

I. It may receive complaints of a refusal of justice on the part of the state courts. The decision must be based upon, and be in accordance with, the constitution and laws of the state in which the case arises. If it be found that justice has been refused or retarded, the Bundesrath has the power, by appropriate measures, to force the state to remedy the wrong.‡ If the state courts are, however, by state law incompetent to decide the case on which the claim is based, the claim is invalid, as there is obviously, under the circumstances, no refusal of justice.

---

* Laband, I., 246. An example summarized by Laband (I., 246, note 1) will serve as an illustration of this side of the Bundesrath's activity. During the session of February 27th, 1871, the President of the Bundesrath announced that a difference of opinion had become apparent between the Federal Chancellor's Office (Bundeskanzleramt) and the Senate of Bremen, as to whether an order issued in Bremen forbidding peddling, was or was not in harmony with the imperial law relating to industries. The matter was, at the suggestion of the President, referred to the IV. Committee to be reported upon. The committee decided that the order was in opposition to the objects of the federal law. The Plenipotentiary of Bremen thereupon declared that the Senate of his city would repeal the order in question.

† See Laband, I., 247. The decision which devolves on the Bundesrath in regard to the federal *execution* is judicial in its nature. .

‡ Schulze, Deut. Staatsr., II., 63–4. Laband, 248. Cons. Art. 77, f.; the clause of the constitution which treats this subject is copied from the 29th Art. of the *Wiener Schlussacte.*

II. The Bundesrath is also empowered by the constitution, (Art. 76, 1) to decide, on the appeal of one of the parties, cases arising between different members of the union, so far as they are not simply civil cases falling within the jurisdiction of the regular courts. This is only a species of last resort, a means to promote the possibility of a peaceful solution of difficulties, for war between the conflicting states is of course absolutely excluded.*

III. Finally, Article 76, 2, of the Constitution confers upon the Bundesrath a power, to say the least, somewhat startling in its nature—that of arbitration when difficulties of a constitutional character arise between the different factors of the state governments. The clause reads, "In case of conflicts of a constitutional nature in states where there is no appointed authority to decide such matters, the Bundesrath shall, upon the application of one of the parties, settle the difficulty amicably. If this does not succeed, the matter shall be disposed of with the forms of federal legeslation."† It is to be observed that the Bundesrath is to interfere only when appealed to by one of the parties concerned. Should the conflict, however, be of a nature to prevent the fulfilment of the duties of the state towards the federation, the Bundesrath (in accordance with article 19 of the constitution relating to the *execution*) has the right to interpose without being called upon. Farther, where the throne in

---

* Recognizing the unfitness of the Bundesrath to act in this capacity, Martitz (l. c., p. 37) observes : "Man wird kaum umhin können, nach dem Vorgange der nordamerikanischen und schweizerischen Verfassung auch für die norddeutsche Union ein Bundesgericht mit der Aburtheilung der Streitigkeiten zwischen den Bundesgliedern zu betrauen." See also Seydel, Holzendorff, and Brentano's *Jahrbuch*, III., 288, ff.

† "Verfassungsstreitigkeiten in solchen Bundesstaaten, in deren Verfassung nicht eine Behörde zur Entscheidung solcher Streitigkeiten bestimmt ist, hat auf Anrufen eines Theiles, der Bundesrath gütlich auszugleichen, oder, wenn das nicht gelingt, im Wege der Reichsgesetzgebung zur Erledigung zu bringen."

a state is the object of contention between two or more pretenders, the Bundesrath not only may, but must exert an influence on the outcome, inasmuch as the rights of membership in the Empire are exercised by the head of the state. The Bundesrath would be forced to decide which aspirant to the throne was entitled to be represented in its midst by his plenipotentiaries.

Conflicts of a constitutional nature are very apt to be directly and indirectly connected with a misunderstanding between the monarch and his subjects, or, more specifically, between the cabinet (Regierung) and the representatives of the people. In the decision of a case of this character, the Bundesrath is obviously no impartial judge. It is itself an assembly of rulers, and possesses all the prejudices of rulers. Where the sympathies of the arbitrator would be, is clear. The influence its members might exert on one of their own number, in their attempt amicably to bring about an understanding, would be neutralized by the well-founded suspicion with which an angry parliament would view their intervention. Thus it is expedient that ultimately a counterbalancing factor, the Reichstag, should be called in, or, as the Constitution expresses it, that the decision of the question should take the form of a legislative act. Composing this bicameral court we have, on the one hand, the plenipotentiaries of the Bundesrath, voting according to the instructions of the monarchs, whose brother ruler is involved, on the other hand, the representatives of the people, influenced by a variety of political tendencies and ready to defend their fellow representatives in the state. As Laband says,* when two such bodies are called upon to exercise the functions of a court of justice, for which they are in no way adapted, and attempt to agree upon a verdict, the probability that the motives of the. decision will be of a purely judicial character is extremely small. The consti-

---

* Page 232.

tution does not, in fact, require that the decision should have a judicial character.

The solution of the difficulty may take the form of a change of the state constitution, or of an annulling of that portion of the constitutional law of the state which gave rise to the conflict. For Article 2 of the imperial Constitution, which declares that federal law takes precedence of the state laws, applies to a case of legislation based on the clause we have been considering, by which the existing law of one of the states is modified by the Empire.*

The moral of all this, which is not likely to escape a citizen of the United States, is formulated by probably the most distinguished authority on German constitutional law, as follows: "A consideration of this clause yields two significant results: first, it is apparent that the individual state is not sovereign in the field left to it, but the Empire stands above it, in reality the highest power, in truth the real sovereign; secondly, it is obvious from the functions of the organs of the Empire, in particular those exercised by the Bundesrath, that legislation, administration and justice are not sharply defined departments, but are simply forms in which the one and indivisible power of the state manifests itself."†

---

* Laband, 252.

† Laband, 252. This power of interfering with the state constitutions is sharply criticized by Martitz in his suggestive little book on the North German Constitution (Betrachtungen über die Verfassung des Norddeutschen Bundes 1868). But while he calls the provisions on this matter "*in hohem grade bedenklich,*" and asserts that "der gesammte verfassungsmässige Rechtszustand der deutschen Staaten in Frage-gestellt wird" (pp. 29 and 31) he admits that "der Bund den Verfas-sungsconflikten der Einzelstaaten schlecterdings nicht gleichgiltig gegenüberstehen kann, dass ihm in jedem Falle die Möglichkeit gewährt werden muss, denselben die gefährlichen Spitzen abzu-schneiden, diese Nothwendigkeit bedarf keines Erweises." In other words, this contingent interference with the affairs of the individual state is a tradition so deeply rooted in the German mind that even the liberal thinkers cannot free themselves from it. A further example is to be found in the liberal constitution of 1848-9.

The preceding study ought, it seems to me, to help us to a truer view of the real nature of our own government. As we have seen, the German Constitution was not the product of abstract political speculation, but was strictly conditioned, at its formation, by existing national traditions and by the specific demands of the moment. We find in it no room for institutions copied from other federal systems. It is relative to the German nation, purely indigenous, and hence, *sui generis*. But is not the same true of our own form of government? Have the principles enunciated in the *Federalist*, for example, a universal applicability, or are they, to a much greater extent than we are wont to suppose, simply rules for a single nation, at a particular period of its development? We may seek an answer to this question in two directions. We may investigate the origin of our constitution, and determine whether or no its founders were governed in their work, by a desire to realize abstract ideals, or were contented, in the main, to adopt such arrangements as were sanctioned by the experience of the states. Or we may compare our constitution with other examples of federal organizations, and see whether there be a unity running through them all which would justify us in assigning an absolute value to those rules which have been observed in the formation of our own federation. In respect to the origin of the constitution of the United States, I have attempted to show in a previous article,[*] that our existing form of government had a much more gradual development than is generally supposed. The work of the Convention of 1787 consisted chiefly in what may be called the federalizing of the political institutions of the individual states, even the original features being strictly in harmony with the national traditions. The second method by which it seems possible to reach a solution of the problem suggested above, we have pur-

---

[*] The Original and Derived Features of the Constitution. Annals of the Am. Acad. of Political and Social Science, Oct., 1890.

sued in the foregoing pages. The result is clear. We have found upon studying the constitution of the chief example of a federal state in Europe, that it is not formed according to the same plan as that of the United States. The German Federation is, as De Tocqueville once said of our own union, in reality, a new thing with an old name. In attempting to study it with our national preconceptions, we find ourselves at first baffled by the constant disregard of the formulations of our classical works on politics. It is only when we recognize the possibility of independent constitutional development in lines wholly different from those which the United States has followed, and cease to try to classify all political phenomena according to a system applicable in general only to our own national evolution, that we begin to perceive the real nature of the German Imperial Constitution. But if, as we seem warranted in concluding, the political institutions of a nation must be relative to its social and economic status, the attempt to lay down general principles of government applicable to every country, or even to a single country in every stage of its development, must always prove futile. Every nation is, however, in a constant state of flux. Our own, in particular, has undergone the most profound changes since the close of the last century, and we have, perhaps, cause to envy the good fortune of those countries where the constitution is not so rigid as to preclude a more or less unconscious readjustment between the political institutions and the constantly changing social and economic life of the nation.

www.ingramcontent.com/pod-product-compliance
Lightning Source LLC
Chambersburg PA
CBHW021534270326
41930CB00008B/1252